Wolfgang Jarastch

Stevie Leach

Steven Leach

Science for Work and Play
Science for Here and Now
Science Far and Near
Science in Your Life
Science in Our World
Science for Today and Tomorrow

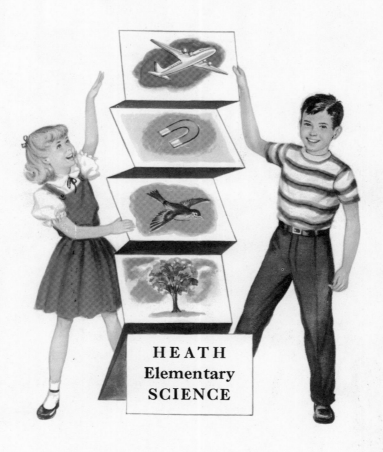

HEATH
Elementary
SCIENCE

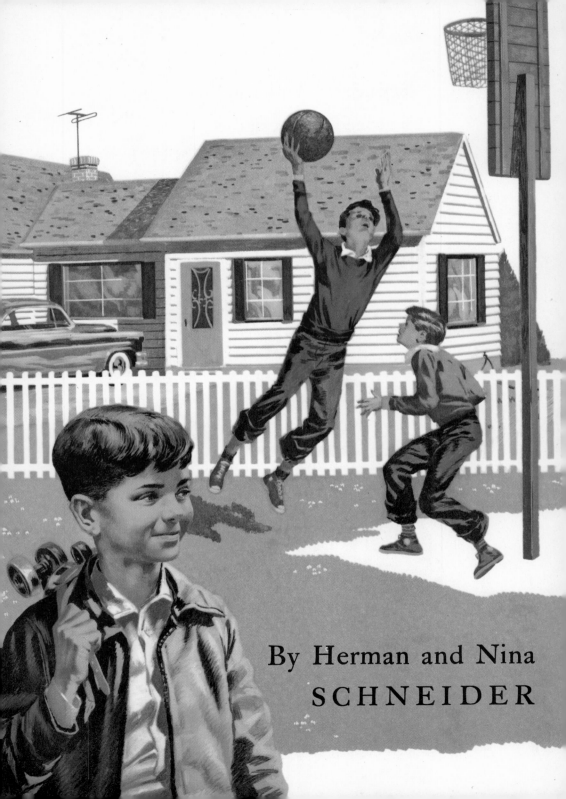

By Herman and Nina
SCHNEIDER

SCIENCE
in Your Life

D. C. HEATH AND COMPANY

Copyright, 1955, by D. C. HEATH AND COMPANY   Printed in the U. S. A.   (5 B 7)

CONTENTS

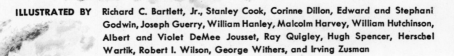

ILLUSTRATED BY Richard C. Bartlett, Jr., Stanley Cook, Corinne Dillon, Edward and Stephani Godwin, Joseph Guerry, William Hanley, Malcolm Harvey, William Hutchinson, Albert and Violet DeMee Jousset, Ray Quigley, Hugh Spencer, Herschel Wartik, Robert I. Wilson, George Withers, and Irving Zusman

What kind of weather are you having right now? Is it raining? Is it snowing? Is it hot or cold, calm or windy? Perhaps you are watching an exciting lightning storm. Perhaps hailstones are clattering on the roof. You may be having any one of many kinds of weather.

Perhaps you do not like the kind of weather you are having right now. Would you like to have different weather? All you would have to do is go somewhere else.

Somewhere else the weather is warm and pleasant. In another place snow is falling. In still other places lightning is flashing and thunder crashing.

Hail, sleet, clear, cloudy! In this one world you can find hundreds of different kinds of weather right now!

So many different kinds of weather in one world! How can it be hot and cold, rainy and dry, windy and calm, all at once?

We can find out about some of the things that make the weather.

How Heat Makes the Weather

When you walk barefoot on a hot sandy beach, your feet feel hot.

The heat of the sand makes them feel hot. Where did the heat of the sand come from?

It came from the sun. The sun shining on the sand makes it hot.

The sun heats the land and the water and the air of the earth. It heats the plants and the people and everything it shines on. The sun gives the heat for all the weather in the world.

The Sun Warms the Earth

You know that the earth is a huge ball that turns in the sunlight. As each part of the earth turns into the sunlight, it becomes daytime in that part.

Sun's rays

Earth

As each part turns away from the sunlight into darkness, it becomes nighttime. At night only the stars, and sometimes the moon, send a little light to us.

Into the sunlight and daytime, then into darkness and nighttime, the earth keeps turning all the time.

When your part of the earth turns into the sunlight, everything begins to warm up. All day long the land is warmed by the sun. The water and the air are warmed, too; all the things around you, and even you, yourself, are warmed by the sun.

Then your part of the earth turns away from the sunlight, and everything begins to cool as night comes.

Sun

With a globe and a light you can see how day and night follow each other. Find your city on the globe, and watch it as you slowly turn the globe.

Cold and Warm Sunny Days

It is daytime every day, but the weather is not the same every day. A bright, sunny day in winter is not so warm as a bright, sunny day in summer. It is the same sun shining. What makes the difference?

Do this experiment to see that more sunlight makes more heat.

EXPERIMENT

Get two saucers of water.

Put one in bright sunlight and leave it there for ten minutes.

Then put another saucer of water next to it. Leave both saucers in the sunlight for another minute.

Now one saucer has had sunlight for eleven minutes and the other for only one minute.

Touch the water in both saucers. Which feels warmer?

Try the same experiment, using a thermometer.

You will find that the water that was in the sunlight for eleven minutes is warmer than the water in the other saucer. Time in the sunlight made the difference.

Time in the sunlight makes a difference in the kind of weather you have.

In the summer the sun shines for many hours every day. When you get up early in the morning and look outside, the sun is already there, shining away, warming everything.

All through the day, for as much as fourteen to sixteen hours in the United States, the sun keeps shining on you and everything around you. Things can become quite warm in as many hours of bright sunlight as that.

Summer

JULY
4

Winter

DEC
25

In the winter the sun does not shine for so many hours each day. It rises later and sets earlier, so that it shines for only about nine hours in many parts of the United States. With fewer hours of sunlight, there is less time for everything to be warmed.

Summer

Winter

Lots of sunlight can make the weather hot. The weather is usually cooler when there is less sunlight. That is one reason why we have different kinds of weather.

Was it light when you awoke this morning?

Did you go to bed when it was dark last night, or was there still light?

Cloudy and Cool

When the sky is full of clouds, the weather feels cooler. You know that the sun is there. It is hidden by the clouds. Why does this change the weather?

You can find out with a sheet of black paper.

EXPERIMENT

Fold the black paper in half. Put it in the sunlight, on a book that has been in the shade.

After five minutes, touch each half.

Which feels cooler?

Try the same experiment, using a thermometer. The shaded part is cooler because the sunlight was blocked off.

In the same way, when clouds block off some of the sunlight, the land is not heated so much as on a sunny day.

A cloudy day is usually cooler than a sunny day.

Cooler near the Water

Do you like to go swimming on a hot day? You know how cool and pleasant the water feels. Even if you do not go into the water, you usually feel cool near the water.

The air is usually cooler there than it is away from the water. The same sun shines on the beach as on the land that is not near the water. But the air is cooler near the water. The air over the cool water is cooler than the air over the hot land. Why is the water cooler than the land on a hot day?

Perhaps water does not heat up so quickly as land. We can find out.

EXPERIMENT

Put some dry soil into a dish. This will be the land.

Pour water into another dish of the same size. If the water is very cold, add warm water until it is as warm as the soil.

Now put both dishes in a sunny place and leave them there for ten minutes.

Which one has warmed up more in the sunlight?

You can use a thermometer to find out.

Do you find that the soil is warmer?

Soil heats up more quickly than water and so do most other materials. The streets and houses of a city and the soil and rocks of the country all heat up more quickly than water.

The water stays cool, and it helps to keep the air cool, too. Some of the cool air over the water moves to the nearby land where you sit and say, "Ah, how cool!"

The Beach at Night

In your experiment you found that in the sunlight the land heats up more quickly than the water. That is why the beach may be too hot for your bare feet, at the same time that the water is pleasantly cool. But what happens at night, after the sun goes down?

At night, of course, everything begins to cool off. But which cools off faster — the land or the water? You can find out with a bowl of dry soil and a bowl of water.

EXPERIMENT

First, put the bowl of water and the bowl of dry soil in a warm, shady place. Leave them there until the soil and the water are at the same temperature. Use a thermometer to test the temperature.

Now you are ready to find out which one cools off faster. Put both bowls in a refrigerator for about fifteen minutes. Then take them out and touch the top of the water.

Which feels cooler? Test the temperature of each with a thermometer.

Did you find that the soil feels cooler than the water? Soil cools off more quickly than water. So do sand, pebbles, and most other materials. After the sun sets, a sandy or pebbly beach cools off quickly. But the water cools off only a little bit.

Perhaps you have found this out for yourself. Have you ever gone wading at the shore on a summer night? As you stepped from the cool beach into the water, you found a surprise. The water was warmer than you expected! It had cooled off only a little bit after sunset, while the sand or pebbles had cooled off much more.

How Heat and Air Make the Weather

You know that wind is moving air. Every wind, whether it is a gentle breeze or a fierce gale, is moving air. But what makes the air move?

The sun does! The winds of the earth are made by the faraway sun. Let's see how.

You know that the sun warms the land and the water of the earth. The air, too, is warmed.

When air is warmed, something happens to it. Here is a way to find out what happens.

EXPERIMENT

You will need a hot plate, a small pan, a balloon, and a baby's bottle. Get the kind of bottle that can be heated without breaking.

Snap the balloon over the neck of the bottle.

Put a little water in the pan. Place the bottle in the pan and put the pan on the hot plate.

The hot water will heat the bottle and the air inside. What happens as the air is heated?

You will see the balloon fill out as air flows into it.

The air came from the bottle. When air is heated it spreads out, or expands. The heated air in the bottle expands into the balloon.

When air is heated, it expands. Some of the air flows out of the bottle when it is heated. Then there is less air in the bottle than before.

A bottle filled with warm air is lighter than a bottle filled with cold air. We can say that warm air is lighter than cold air.

Warm air   Cool air

You know that on a sunny day the land heats up more than the water. The air over the land becomes hotter than the air over the water. The warmer air is lighter than the cooler air over the water.

Warm air   Cool air

When warm, light air meets heavy air, something happens. You can find out what happens by doing an experiment.

EXPERIMENT

You will need two blackboard erasers and an electric lamp with a large bulb.

Light the bulb and wait a minute until it becomes hot. The bulb warms the air around it.

The warm air expands and becomes lighter.

Now there is warm, light air next to the bulb, and cool, heavier air farther away.

Something happens between the two airs.

To see what happens, hold the erasers near the bulb and clap them together to make chalk dust in the air.

You will see chalk dust rising from the erasers.

The dust is being carried up by the warm, rising air. The warm, light air rises as it is pushed up by the cool, heavy air nearby.

A Small Wind

Warm air is pushed up by cold air. This happens whenever warm air and cold air meet.

It happens when a radiator heats the air around it. The heated air expands and becomes lighter. Then the cool, heavy air in the room flows toward it and pushes it up.

When the cool air reaches the radiator, it, too, becomes heated and is pushed up.

Over and over, around and around, the air keeps flowing. This moving air is really a small wind.

There is another way to make a wind in a room. When you open the windows at the top and bottom you allow cold, fresh air to flow in through the bottom. The warm, stale air is pushed up and out through the top. You can see this for yourself in this experiment.

EXPERIMENT

Shut the doors and open a window a few inches, top and bottom.

Tack a strip of thin paper to a window pole. Hold it up to the top of an open window.

Which way does it blow?

Now hold it near the bottom.

Which way does it blow?

Tell why this is a good way to air a room.

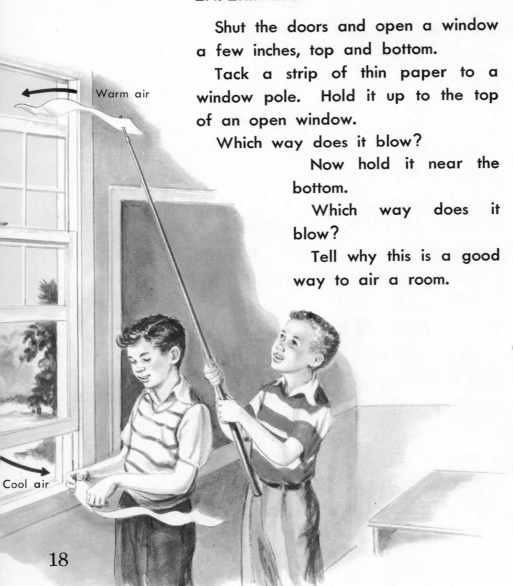

Warm air

Cool air

18

Big and Little Winds

The winds outside your room are also made by the meeting of cool and warm air. At the beach on a sunny day cool air flows in toward the land. It pushes warm air up and out of the way. A cool wind blows across the warm land. This is called a sea breeze.

Warm air

Cool air

At night the breeze flows the other way. You remember that land cools off more quickly than water. At night the air over the land gets cool. The air over the water does not cool so quickly. The cool land air flows out to the water. It pushes the warmer air up and makes a wind. This is called a land breeze.

Warm air

Cool air

Over land and sea we can find winds of many sizes. Little winds drift gently from the cool shade of a tree, from the shady side of a street, from the cool water of a pond.

Cool air from the shady side of a mountain makes a wind as it sweeps down across a sunny valley and pushes the warm air upward.

Cool air

Warm air

Where the cool air is just a little cooler than the warm air next to it, the breeze is gentle. Where there is a big difference between the warm air and the cool air, the wind is strong.

As you can see, the sun is really the cause of winds. Without the sun, the air would not be heated. The air is heated more in some places than in other places. Because of this, we have little breezes and big winds.

The sun's heat makes the winds of the world.

Water in the Weather

Rain, fog, snow, mist, clouds, hail, sleet, frost, and dew. Here are nine different words that are alike in one way. They all have to do with water in the weather.

How are these things different? Why does water sometimes fall in the form of rain and other times as snow? And how did water become clouds?

Let's find out about water in the weather.

Where Is the Water?

You know that wet clothes dry when they are hung out on a line. You know that puddles dry after the rain. Where does the water go when things dry? Here is a way to find out.

EXPERIMENT

Get two clean, dry glass jars with tops.

Pour about a quarter of an inch of water into one jar. Be careful not to wet the sides.

Then cover both jars and put them in the sunlight or some other warm place. Let them stand for a half hour or so.

Do you see a misty film of water on the sides of the jar that has water in it? You may even see a few drops of water on the side and under the cover. Is there any water film in the other jar?

The water drops came from the water in the first jar. The water evaporated into the air in the jar. It became water vapor. Then the water vapor formed drops of liquid water on the sides and top of the jar.

When the water vapor forms drops of water, we say it condenses.

Up, Up, Up!

You cannot see the water evaporate, because it goes up in very tiny particles, as water vapor. These particles are water but they are so small that they cannot be seen.

We call these tiny particles molecules. "Molecule" is the name we give to the smallest possible particles of a substance, such as water.

Evaporation is going on everywhere in the world. Helped by the sun's heat, water evaporates from oceans and rivers, from pools and puddles, from damp leaves and damp faces.

Up, up into the sun-warmed air, the molecules of water vapor keep rising and rising.

Down, Down, Down!

Whatever goes up comes down. The millions of molecules of water vapor that go up into the air do not stay there forever.

They come down in many ways, in many shapes and sizes. You can make them come down yourself. Here is how.

EXPERIMENT

Put some ice cubes and water in a clean, dry jar. Cover the jar and let it stand. Soon you will see a misty film of water on the outside.

Look closely and you will see that the film is made of little drops of water.

Touch them and feel how wet they are.

These drops were formed from water vapor in the air near the jar.

When water vapor is cooled, it collects into little drops of water.

Now wait a little longer. You will see the little drops roll together and form bigger drops.

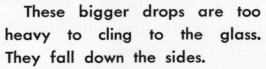

These bigger drops are too heavy to cling to the glass. They fall down the sides.

You have made water vapor come out of the air, form into drops, and fall down.

Clouds

In your experiment you used ice cubes to cool the water vapor in the room air. The drops collected on the outside of the jar.

In the outside air of the world, water vapor is cooled by cool air and in other ways. The molecules of water vapor, which are too small to be seen, collect into larger drops that can be seen.

When the drops form high in the sky, they make up a cloud. You cannot see each separate drop in the cloud, of course, because you are too far away. But you do see the whole cloud.

You could not see separate drops on the cold jar either, until you came closer. If you go into a cloud in an airplane, you see drops of water form on the window and run down just as they did on the cold jar.

Fog

Water vapor sometimes forms a cloud near the ground. We call such a cloud, fog.

In a fog everything seems wrapped in a soft cloud. Cars and boats slow down as they go through it. You can see the separate drops of water on windowpanes and cars. Everything looks wet. You can feel the wetness of fog as it clings to your face and hands.

Dew

In your experiment with the jar and ice cubes, you saw little drops of water collect on the cool jar.

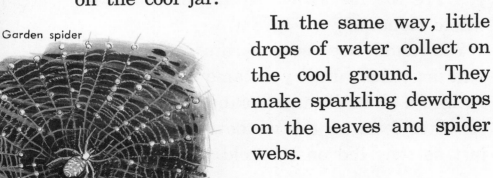

Garden spider

In the same way, little drops of water collect on the cool ground. They make sparkling dewdrops on the leaves and spider webs.

Rain

Sometimes the sky is cloudy day after day. It seems as though the clouds will stay forever. Then at last it rains.

Even scientists do not know the whole story of how rain is formed. Perhaps some-day we shall find out exactly how it is formed. However, we do know that when clouds become cooler and cooler the little drops of water of which they are made come closer and closer together. Often they act like the drops on your cooled jar and form bigger drops.

The bigger drops are too heavy to stay up. Down they come as raindrops!

The water that went up as water vapor, which you could not see or feel, comes splashing down as rain.

Sleet

Sometimes raindrops fall through very cold air. They freeze as they fall.

Frozen rain comes down as sleet, pattering against windows, clicking on pavements.

Drops of sleet are frozen water, like tiny ice cubes.

Hail

Sometimes a strange thing happens to the icy drops of sleet. A strong wind blowing upward catches them. It carries them up into the clouds again.

A layer of water forms on each drop of sleet. Then the drops fall through cold air and the water freezes.

Now there is ice around ice.

Again and again the drops fall and are blown high again.

More and more layers of ice form, until the drops are too heavy to be lifted by the wind, and then they smash to the ground. These heavy pieces of ice are hail. A hailstone is like an ice cube on which you pour water and then put the ice cube and the water back to freeze again.

Down come the hailstones, banging on the roof, clattering on cars, bouncing off your head. Large hailstones are dangerous. Sometimes they can kill small animals in a pasture. If hailstones fall on a field, they can batter crops and heads. This farmer had better get to the barn in a hurry.

Snow

Around the tiny drops of water in a cloud there is water vapor. When the cloud becomes very cold, the water vapor often comes together very quickly. Instead of cooling into raindrops, it freezes into snowflakes.

Snowflakes have many lovely shapes, but you will find that they all have six points.

Perhaps you live in a place where the weather is always warm. Then you may never have seen snow falling. But you can see real snowflakes in your home.

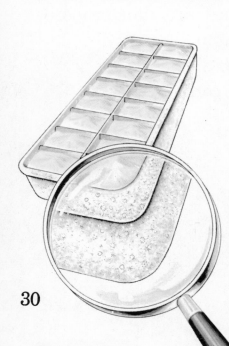

Just open the door of your refrigerator. On the part that holds the trays of ice cubes you can see a white frost.

Look closely and you will see that it is made of many little white snow-flakes, one on top of the other.

These flakes were formed by the freezing of water vapor. When this happens in a refrigerator or on a windowpane, we call it frost. When it happens high up in a cloud, we call it snow.

The Travels of Water

How many different shapes water can take! How many ways it travels up and down and around the world!

The heat of the sun lifts it high into the air. The winds of the world carry it high up and far away. It cools and becomes clouds or fog or dew. It falls as rain, sleet, hail, or snow. It fills lakes and oceans. It soaks into the soil where the roots of plants take it in. Animals drink it. People use it in many ways.

Up, down, and around the world, the travels of water are never over.

Things to Talk About

1. Talk about the different kinds of weather you have had in the past week.

2. Tell how the hours of sunlight make a difference in the weather.

3. Tell why the air is usually cooler near the water in the daytime.

4. Talk about heavy air and lighter air.

5. Talk about the travels of water. What happens to water when it is heated? What happens to water vapor when it is cooled?

Things to Do

1. Listen to weather reports on the radio. Cut some weather reports out of the newspaper.

2. Keep a class weather chart. Show weather conditions, as in the chart below.

WEATHER RECORD					
Date	Oct. 6	Oct. 7	Oct. 8	Oct. 9	Oct. 10
Time	11:00	11:05	11:00		
Outdoor temperature	58°	61°	63°		
Sky condition	Clear	Partly cloudy	Very cloudy		
Rain or snow	No	No	Rain		
Wind direction	NW	W	SW		
Wind speed	Gentle	Moderate	Strong		

3. Go on a trip to the nearest body of water. Take a thermometer with you. Keep a record of the temperature at different places along the way.

Things to Find Out

1. Find out what time the sun rises and what time it sets on your birthday. Find out the times of sunrise and sunset on some important holidays.

2. Find out some of the things these people do when the weather report tells them that a sudden cold wave is coming: a farmer, a house owner, a mother, a car owner, a clothing-store man, a man who sells fuel.

MOVING THINGS ON LAND

Every day is moving day for you. Every day you do all kinds of moving jobs. You carry packages, pull wagons, ride a bicycle, travel in cars and buses, and move around on your own two feet.

All over the world people have moving jobs to do. They bring food from farms to cities. They move goods from factories to stores. Right in your own classroom, everything that you see was brought by somebody.

The chairs and tables, the books and pencils, the building itself — you have all these things because they were moved from far and near. Some things were carried on trucks and trains, others on boats, and some perhaps by airplanes.

On land and sea and through the air, the moving jobs go on all the time, all over the world. Moving is such an important part of the world's work that many people have worked at finding ways of making moving easier and faster.

Over Ice and Snow

On hard, smooth ice and soft, white snow, an Eskimo sled is the way to go. Pulled by powerful Huskies, the sled glides easily on its smooth runners.

Wherever we go on ice or snow, we find ways of gliding. With sleds and skis and skates, we can skim along quickly and silently.

On your mark! Get set! But no, it won't go! The dogs are pulling as hard as they can, but nothing moves. The sled is the same, but the road is different. What makes the difference?

Is it hardness? The road is hard, but so is ice.

Is it softness? Snow is soft, but so is sand.

Is it smoothness? We know that both snow and ice are smooth. Perhaps smoothness makes the difference. We can find out.

EXPERIMENT

Fasten a piece of string to a block of wood. Put a few books on the block. Pull the block over a smooth, shiny board or piece of glass. Then pull it over a rough board. Is it easier to move over the smooth surface? Does smoothness make a difference?

You will find that it is easier to pull the block over the smooth surface.

Is it more work to pull, push, or drag a load over a rough surface than over a smooth surface?

You can do another experiment to see why it is harder work to pull a load over a rough surface than over a smooth surface.

EXPERIMENT

You will need a piece of the finest sandpaper, a rough piece of stone, a rough board, a mirror or a piece of glass, and some fluffy cotton for this experiment. Rub the piece of cotton across the rough surfaces. You will see bits of cotton torn away.

Now rub the piece of cotton across the smooth glass. No cotton sticks to the smooth surface of the glass.

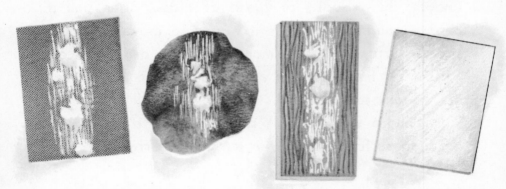

The rough surfaces have many little bumps and hollows and splinters. These rough places catch and drag and tear at the cotton.

This catching and dragging is called friction. There is a great deal of friction between a heavy load and a rough road. There is less friction between a heavy load and a smooth road.

Getting Rid of Friction

In every moving job, friction makes a difference. When you have to drag something over a rough surface, you must pull against lots of friction. This is hard work.

When there is less friction the work is easier. Nobody likes to do things the hard way if there is an easier way. People have found many ways of making moving jobs easier by getting rid of some of the friction.

They use sandpaper, polish, and wax on rough things to make them smooth. The sandpaper rubs the bumps down smooth. The wax and polish cover the surface with a smooth coat.

How does smoothness help in each of these places?

People who live in snow-covered lands have smooth roads all ready for them to use. There is a problem with snow roads, though. If you crunch into snow, it is easily made rough and full of holes. Walking in snow

and carrying loads is not easy work. To move over smooth snow and ice surfaces, people have made many things that slide over snow and ice with very little friction.

Safety on Ice

Traveling on snow and ice is fun because you glide along easily. There is very little friction to hold you back. For the same reason, we need to be sure that the gliding is done in places where you do not have to stop suddenly. You need friction for a quick stop, and there is very little friction on snow and ice.

Tell how knowing about friction can help you to play safely on snow and ice.

Over Dry Land

Gliding and sliding are fine across snow and ice. But in many parts of the world there is no snow and ice. In such places people have found that it is usually easier to move things by rolling than by dragging.

You can see why rolling is easier than dragging if you do this experiment.

EXPERIMENT

First you drag the round block through the sand.

Now you roll the block. Which is easier?

You can feel that it is easier to roll than to drag.

When you drag something, it pushes through bumps that rub and grip. It pushes some of the sand out of the way. When you drag, there is a great deal of friction.

When you roll something, there is much less friction. You travel over the bumps rather than through them. The bumps do not hold you back so much. On a rough surface, rolling is easier than sliding or dragging.

Here are loads on their own rollers.

Here are rollers being used to move some very heavy things.

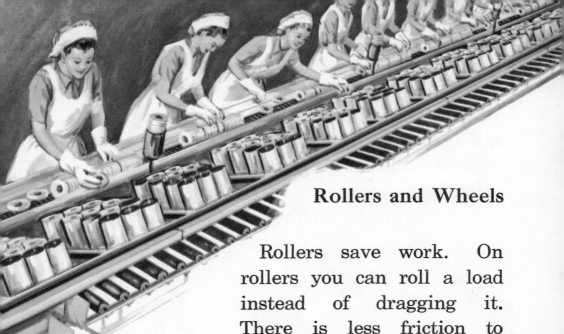

Canning pineapples

Rollers and Wheels

Rollers save work. On rollers you can roll a load instead of dragging it. There is less friction to work against.

In the picture below you can see that there is a problem with rollers. Somebody has to follow the load and pick up each roller as it is left behind.

Each roller, in turn, must be picked up and brought to the front of the load.

Just imagine delivering a load of lumber this way! How do you think the school bus would work on rollers?

We need to attach the rollers so that they will stay with the load. How can we do this?

It is not easy to attach a big, heavy roller; so let's cut it into slices. These slices will be wheels.

Now let's bore a hole in each wheel.

Then put a thin pole through the pair of wheels. This pole is called an axle.

The wheels turn around on the axle.

If we attach a box to the axle, we have a two-wheeled cart, such as this.

Less Friction in Wheels

Wheels are better than rollers. You remember that rollers have to be picked up and carried forward. Wheels stay with the load. But wheels have a special problem.

You can see what this problem is by making a wheel of your own.

EXPERIMENT

Cut a wheel out of cardboard, or use the top of a round carton. Make a hole in the center. The hole should be large enough to let a pencil fit loosely.

Hold the pencil and spin the wheel.

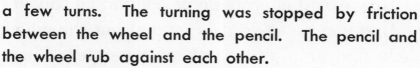

You will find that the wheel does not spin long. It stops after a few turns. The turning was stopped by friction between the wheel and the pencil. The pencil and the wheel rub against each other.

In a wagon that carries a load, there is rubbing between the wheel and the axle in addition to the friction between the rolling wheel and the road. This rubbing between the wheel and the axle makes it harder work to pull the wagon. It also rubs away tiny bits of the wheel and the axle. Friction causes the wheel and the axle to wear. The heavier the load, the more wearing away takes place. The axle may wear away so much that it will finally break.

47

How can this problem of friction be solved?

One way to solve it is by making the wheel hole and axle as smooth as possible. There is little friction between two smooth things.

However, between the smoothest wheel hole and axle there is some friction. Even this little friction slows down the wheels and wears away the wood. The smoothest material we can make still has some bumps. They are very tiny bumps but they rub.

If these bumps can be kept from touching, there will be less friction.

We can keep them from touching by covering the surfaces with something. You can see how.

EXPERIMENT

Rub two crisp pieces of toast together.

Listen to them crackle and grate as they rub.

Now spread a thick layer of butter over the slices.

Rub them together again.

Do you hear anything?

When we cover two surfaces with a thin layer of oil or grease, it keeps them from rubbing against each other. When the materials do not touch, they cannot rub. There is less friction.

If we put oil or grease between a wheel and an axle, there is less friction.

You can see how oil helps.

EXPERIMENT

Get an old wagon.

Make a chalk mark on the side of one wheel.

Spin the wheel and count the turns it makes before stopping.

Listen to the rattling and squeaking as the rough spots rub against each other.

Now oil the place where the axle and the wheel touch each other.

The film of oil will spread. It will cover the rough places that rubbed against each other.

Now spin the wheel and see how many turns it makes before stopping. Does it squeak less?

There is less friction because the wheel glides around on a film of oil. We say the oil lubricates the wheel. The lubricated wheel does not rub and drag so much. Lubrication is used to reduce friction in many machines.

In things as tiny as a wrist watch and as huge as an ocean liner, lubrication helps the parts move more easily and smoothly.

Ball Bearings

Good, better, and still better! Plain wheels are good for moving a load. Oiled and greased wheels are better because they spin with less friction. There is an even better kind of wheel that turns with still less friction. It is used in bicycles and roller skates.

It is called a ball-bearing wheel, because it has little balls rolling against the axle. Let's see how these rolling balls help make rolling still easier.

EXPERIMENT

You will need about fifteen or twenty marbles, all of the same size. You will also need a heavy book and a coffee-can lid which has a rim.

Put the book on the floor and try to spin it. It will not spin well. What stops it? You know that there is friction between the book and the floor.

51

Put the marbles on the floor and cover them with the lid. Now spin the book on the lid.

Can you see how the rolling balls made it easier? Watch them roll around as they carry the load. When you try to spin the book by itself, there is dragging and friction between the book and the floor.

When you spin the book over the balls, there is less friction. The balls do not drag; they roll.

The same thing happens in the wheels of bicycles and roller skates.

These wheels are built with a ring of steel balls between the axle and the wheel. They roll as the wheel turns and keep the wheel from rubbing against the axle. Such a wheel is called a ball-bearing wheel because the weight of the load bears down on a ring of balls around the axle.

Ball-bearing wheels help you speed along quickly and easily on skates or on a bicycle. A car has them in many places, and so does a train. All kinds of machines, big and little, use this fine way of changing a dragging motion to a rolling motion.

At an auto repair shop you can get old ball bearings free. Mount them on a chart, showing in what part of the car they were used. If you have old ball bearings from roller skates, bicycles, or other machines, add them to your chart.

Do We Need Friction?

Rollers, wheels, lubrication, ball bearings — how are all these alike? They are all ways of helping to get rid of friction.

They all help to make moving easier by making less friction. If we could get rid of all friction, would the work of moving loads be very, very easy? Before you make up your mind, try this experiment.

EXPERIMENT

Get a jar with a screw top, a piece of soap, and a dish of water.

Screw the cover on the jar as tightly as you can. Then unscrew it.

Once again screw the cover on tightly.

You are able to do these things because there is friction between your hands and the jar.

Now let's try the same work with less friction. Wet your hands with soapy water and then try to unscrew the cover. Can you do it?

Perhaps you can, but your hands will slip because they are wet. It will be quite a struggle.

You will miss your helper, friction.

Friction is useful to you in hundreds of different ways every day. You are able to walk because there is friction between your shoes and the ground. You know how you slip and slide with new shoes on a smooth floor.

Without friction the wheels of a car would spin without moving the car.

If somehow the car did get moving, you would really be in trouble, because you could not stop. The brakes of a car are made of materials that stop the wheels by friction when the driver presses the brake pedal.

GO

STOP

In every kind of travel you start and stop by friction. Is it easier to start and stop on wet days? Why must you be very, very careful when crossing streets on wet days?

Are you sitting in a chair right now? If there were no friction you would slide off every time you wiggled. Are you holding this book in your hand? What keeps it from sliding out of your hand? Did you write with a pencil or chalk today? You were able to write because friction tears away bits of pencil or chalk and these bits stick to the paper or blackboard.

Just look around you and think of the things you did in the last ten minutes. Could you have done them without friction?

Things to Talk About

1. Can you stop your bicycle more quickly on a wet road or on a dry road? Why?

2. Tell why tires wear out faster on a rough road than on a smooth road.

3. Tell why good roads are not as smooth as glass.

4. Would you put smooth tiles or rough tiles around a swimming pool? On which would it be easier to slip and fall?

5. What does each of these pictures tell about friction?

Things to Do

1. Find wheels that make work easy in the classroom. You may find them in rolling doors, in window shades, and in other places.

2. Make a display of toys and models showing ways of moving things on land.

3. Look at a door hinge. Find the surfaces that rub against each other. How would you take the squeak out of a door hinge?

4. Bicycles, roller skates, sewing machines, watches, and cars are lubricated with different kinds of lubricants. Make a collection of some different kinds of lubricants.

5. Make a friction chart. In one part put things that are useful because they have lots of friction. In another part put things that are useful because they have little friction. Use real objects whenever possible to make the chart interesting.

6. Make a class mural showing land travel from early times until today.

Things to Find Out

1. Find out the meanings of these words: Conestoga wagon, travois, sedan chair, caravan, chaise.

2. Find out how a bicycle brake works. Explain it to the class.

3. Find out about roller bearings. How are they different from ball bearings?

MOVING IN WATER

In the world of water, many things go traveling. Some travel by muscle power. Some go with engines that turn wheels and propellers. Some travel along the top of the water, while others go deep down beyond the reach of daylight. Some are living things and others were made by living things.

Yet here is a strange fact. All things that travel in the water under their own power travel in the same way. Whether they move with arms and legs, with tails, or with wheels and propellers, they all really have the same way of moving. You know about this way if you know how to swim.

Swimming

You swim by reaching your arms forward and pushing against the water. As you push against the water, you move some of the water backward. You cause yourself to move forward.

The same push moves the water backward and yourself forward. To move ahead in the water you have to push backward against something. As you move forward, something must move backward.

No matter what swimming stroke you use, no matter whether you are a good swimmer or just a beginner, you travel forward in the same way. You move yourself forward by pushing backward against the water. You cannot move forward unless there is something to push against, backward.

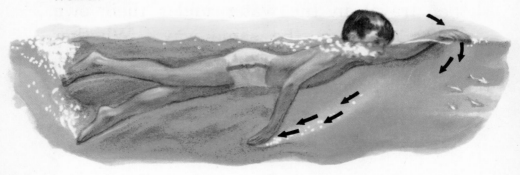

Goldfish

How Water Animals Swim

A fish pushes itself forward with its tail. Watch the fish in your aquarium swinging their way forward through the water. A fish has strong muscles that swing its tail in a curving motion from side to side.

This swinging motion sends water swirling backward as it sends the fish forward.

The squid is a sea animal that moves through the water in a strange way. It has a strong built-in pumping machine under its head that pulls in sea water through a cavity and then forces it out through a tube. The powerful jet of water streaming forward sends the squid backward.

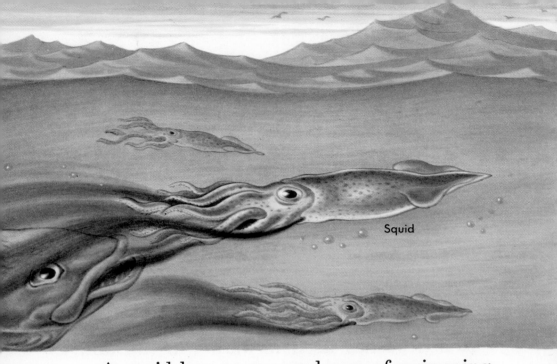

Squid

A squid has an unusual way of swimming, and it can do something even more unusual. It has a little bag of dark-brown ink near the end of its water pump.

When the squid is being chased, it squirts some ink into the jet of water. The water turns a deep, cloudy brown, leaving the hunter puzzled and confused.

How Boats Move

Little rowboats and huge ocean liners, boats with propellers and boats with paddles — there are many kinds of boats, in all shapes and sizes. Yet all of them that move under their own power push their way through the water in the same way. All of them move forward by pushing against the water and moving it backward.

In a canoe you push backward with your paddle. You send a stream of water swirling behind you, and you send the canoe and yourself forward.

In a rowboat you move the boat forward when you push against the water and send a flow of water backward.

Perhaps you have seen pictures of an old-time paddle-wheel boat like this one.

The paddle wheels are like wheels with paddles attached to them.

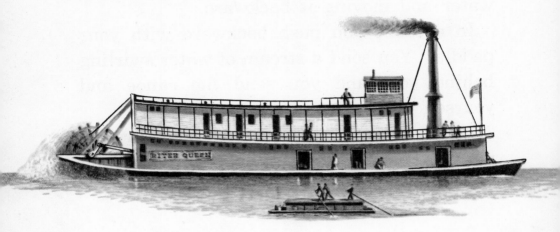

The wheels are turned by a steam engine. Each paddle in turn strikes against the water and pushes it backward.

In this picture, which way does the wheel turn to move the boat forward? Which way does the water flow as the paddles strike it?

Propeller

Paddle wheels are huge things. They take up a lot of space and weigh many tons. Modern ships are driven in a better way, by propellers.

A propeller is not nearly so big as a paddle wheel, and it weighs much less. If you have a toy wind-up boat, you can find out how a propeller works.

First, look at the propeller. It looks like a fan, and it really is a kind of water fan. An ordinary fan pushes air away from it. Let's see whether a water fan pushes water away from it.

EXPERIMENT

Place the toy boat in a tub of water, with the propeller spinning. Watch the water swirl backward as the boat moves forward.

Here is a better way to see how the water moves.

Let a few drops of ink fall behind the propeller. The movement of the ink will help you to see the movement of the water. Which way does the water go? Which way does the boat go?

As you can see, a propeller pushes backward against the water. The push sends the boat forward, and it also sends a stream of water backward.

Now can you tell why there is a swirl of water behind the ship?

EXPERIMENT

You can make a little boat that pushes against the water in a different way — without oars, paddles, paddle wheels, or propellers.

In this boat air pushes against the water. The boat moves forward as the air pushes the water backward.

You will need a milk carton and a balloon. Cut away one of the sides of the carton. Make a hole in the bottom near one of the ends. Put in the balloon so that the neck sticks out of the hole.

Blow up the balloon and put the boat into a pan of water.

Watch the air bubbles push backward against the water, pushing the boat forward.

Of course, huge ocean liners are not pushed forward by air-filled balloons. Your little boat, however, does one thing that the ocean liner does, too. It pushes itself forward by pushing the water backward. All the water travelers have this same way of traveling, except those that sail, which are pushed forward by the wind.

Everywhere in the water world there are the water travelers, big and little. Tiny water bugs, fish of all sizes and shapes, and all kinds of strange animals go darting and scurrying around. Swimmers and rowers and paddlers of canoes go pushing their way through the water. Ships churn by with propellers whirling.

They travel by pushing the water backward and themselves forward.

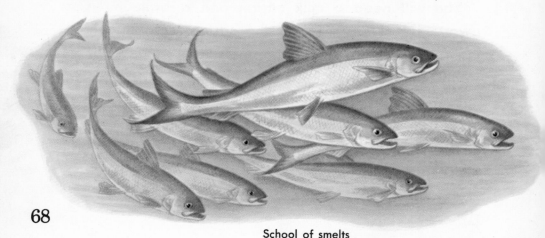

School of smelts

Things to Talk About

1. Tell how you learned to swim.

2. Talk about safety rules for swimmers.

3. Talk about safety rules for using canoes or rowboats.

4. Tell about a boat trip you have taken.

5. Talk about different uses of boats.

Things to Do

1. Lie across a chair and show a swimming stroke that you know how to do. Show how your arms and legs move you forward by pushing back against the water.

2. Make a picture chart of animals that travel through water. Choose pictures that show tails, fins, flippers, legs, webfeet, and other things that the animals use to move through the water.

3. Make a display of model boats. Tell how each kind of boat moves.

4. If boats or parts of boats are made in your community, try to arrange a trip to the boat yard or factory.

5. Show on a globe how a ship would make these voyages: from New York to Florida; from San Francisco to Australia; from the state of Washington to Washington, D.C.

6. Make a class mural called "Water Travel from Log Canoe to Ocean Liner."

Things to Find Out

1. Find out about some insects that live in the water. How do they move through the water?

2. Find out how penguins and seals swim.

3. Find out whether a whale swims in the same way as a fish.

4. Find out about barnacles. How do they make a difference in the speed of a ship?

5. Find out the meanings of these words: bow, stern, fore, aft, port, starboard. What other ship words do you know?

6. Find out about these kinds of boats: kayak, coracle, umiak, outrigger canoe, trireme. How is each kind especially suited to the way it is used?

7. Find out about the steamboat invented by John Fitch. How was it different from Robert Fulton's steamboat?

8. Find out about some foods that are brought to this country from overseas.

RIDING ON AIR

How Birds Fly

When you watch a bird flying, you can almost believe in magic. How wonderful it must be to ride softly on the silent air, high in the sky! The flying of a bird seems very different from the travels of other living things. Flying seems like a very special kind of magic.

Of course, it is not magic. Even though you cannot fly like a bird, you can understand the science of how a bird flies. Even though flying seems very different from walking or crawling or swimming, it is not so different as you might think.

You know how you travel on land. You push against the ground as you walk. It seems hard to believe, but you push the earth a tiny, tiny bit backward as you go forward.

You know how you travel through water. You swim by pushing against the water. You push yourself forward and the water backward.

Flying is a kind of swimming through the air. As a bird flaps its wings, it pushes back against the air. Each push sends it forward a little way. Here is a way to try this yourself.

EXPERIMENT

Put on a pair of roller skates. Then hold two large sheets of heavy cardboard, one in each hand. Put your arms out sideways.

Quickly push backward with your cardboard wings. You will roll forward a few inches.

You moved forward by pushing backward against the air. So does a bird.

Moving forward is not enough for a bird. A bird must get up into the air and stay there. Which way should a bird's wings move to push it up?

When you want to rise from your seat, which way do you push with your arms or legs? Try it and see.

To get up into the air and stay there, a bird pushes down against the air. Each downward flap of its wings pushes the bird up a little way.

At the same time, the bird's wings push backward against the air and send the bird forward. With a curving movement, the wings beat downward and backward. Beat after beat, the bird swims forward and upward through the air.

How People Learned to Fly

It looks so simple! Just keep flapping down and back, down and back. People have always wanted to fly like the birds, and they have built all kinds of airplanes with flapping wings.

They built these flying machines out of wood, out of cloth, and out of many other materials. They even tried feathers.

The machines were of different sizes and shapes, but in one way they were all alike: none of them worked for more than a few seconds.

Was anything wrong? Many things were wrong. One of the things that was wrong was that the wings on the machines were not really like birds' wings.

A bird's wings are not straight and flat. They are not of the same thickness at the front and back. They are not stiff, but can bend and curve as they flap. Nobody has

Great white heron

ever been able to build a wing exactly like those of a bird. Yet only this kind of wing can do both of the flying jobs — keeping up in the air and moving forward.

Suppose we divide the work. Suppose we build a flying machine with one set of parts that keep it up in the air and another set of parts that move it forward.

Some of the early experimenters worked with gliders. A glider stays up in the same way as a kite. That is, it stays up as long as the wind blows against it, or as it is moved through the air.

Other experimenters worked at ways of moving through the air. They tried out propellers to push backward against the air, and engines to turn the propellers.

Finally, Orville and Wilbur Wright made a light engine that could turn a propeller fast enough to pull a glider forward. With wings to keep it up, and with an engine and a propeller to move it forward, the Wright brothers built the first successful man-carrying, engine-driven airplane.

How the Airplane's Propeller Works

You know how a ship's propeller moves a ship forward. The propeller pushes backward against the water and pushes the ship forward.

An airplane's propeller does the same thing in the air. It pushes backward against the air and sends the airplane forward.

Perhaps you have stood behind an airplane on the ground while its propeller was turning. You could feel the strong blast of air being pushed backward by the propeller.

When the propeller is turned fast enough, it begins to pull the airplane forward. The airplane rolls faster and faster.

Now let's find out what makes an airplane rise off the ground and stay up in the air. This is the job of the wings.

How Wings Lift an Airplane

Here is our airplane moving along. We want to get it off the ground into the air. It cannot just float up, because it is much heavier than air.

An airplane needs to be pushed up from underneath. The wings are there to be pushed up, but what can do the pushing? What is under the wings?

There is air under the wings. Can air push up? Let's find out.

EXPERIMENT

You will need a strip of paper about six inches long and two inches wide. Hold it at one end and pull it quickly.

Does the paper rise? What do you think made it rise?

When you pulled the paper quickly, you crowded and squeezed the air under it. This crowded, squeezed air pushed the paper up.

The same thing happens to an airplane rolling quickly along the ground. When it is on the ground, the wings are tipped at a slant, with the front edges higher.

As the plane rolls along, the air under each wing is crowded and squeezed. The air pushes up against the wing. When the plane moves fast enough, the push becomes great enough to lift the plane off the ground.

Push of the air

That is only part of the story. The push of the air under the wings helps to lift the airplane. But we can help this push by clearing the way for it.

There is air on top of the wings, and this air is pushing down. If we can take away some of this downward push, then it will be easier for the air underneath to push up. How can we do this? Here is a way of finding out.

EXPERIMENT

Hold the strip of paper in front of your lips, as shown in the picture, and blow straight across. Do you see the paper rise? You blew straight across the paper.

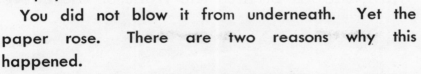

You did not blow it from underneath. Yet the paper rose. There are two reasons why this happened.

First of all, notice that the front of the paper is curved. When your breath hits this curve, the air bounces up a little as it travels across the paper.

Now there is less air right above the paper. There is less air pushing down. This is just what we want. By bouncing away some of the air on top, we have made it possible for the air under the paper to push it up.

Here is another reason why the paper rose. The air you blew across it was moving fast. When air moves forward quickly, it does not push down so hard. That is another thing that makes it easier for the air under the paper to push it up.

If you look at an airplane wing from the side, you will see that it is curved on top. As the propeller pulls the airplane forward, the air strikes the front of the curve.

You have just found out how a curved shape causes the air on top to lose some of its downward push. At the same time, the air under the wing is pushing up.

When the upward push is great enough and the downward push is little enough, the airplane can leave the ground and ride on air.

Happy flying! Happy landing!

Helicopters

A helicopter can do many tricks that make it a very useful flying machine. It can fly forward, like an ordinary airplane. It can also fly straight up and down, backward and sideways, or just stand still in the air.

A helicopter's best trick is that it can fly straight up and straight down. This means that it can take off from almost any place and land on almost any place. A helicopter does not need a big, smooth landing field.

How does a helicopter fly straight up? You know that a helicopter does not have wings like an airplane. Instead, it has something whirling on top. This whirling something is really a very large propeller.

You know that an ordinary airplane has a propeller that pushes backward against the air. This push sends the airplane forward.

The propeller on top of a helicopter pushes down against the air. This push sends the helicopter up.

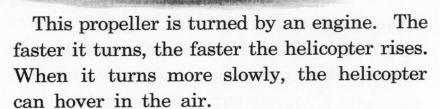

This propeller is turned by an engine. The faster it turns, the faster the helicopter rises. When it turns more slowly, the helicopter can hover in the air.

When the propeller turns still more slowly, the helicopter sinks slowly toward the ground.

How does it move forward? The same propeller takes care of that job. The propeller can be tilted as it turns.

When the propeller is tilted forward a little, the helicopter moves forward. Backward, to the left, to the right — a helicopter will take you any way you want to go.

Airplanes Without Propellers

For anybody who is really in a hurry, jet planes are the way to travel. With a roar and a whistle they streak through the air, faster than the fastest wind. Jet planes have special engines to give them such speed. These are called jet engines.

You know that most airplanes have propellers to pull them through the air. The propellers are turned by engines. Jet planes have a different kind of engine, and no propeller at all!

How can an airplane go without a propeller?
You can find out with a toy balloon.

EXPERIMENT

Blow up the balloon and hold it at the end. Then let it go. Watch the balloon whizz around the room until all the air is out of it.

When you blew up the balloon and held the end, the air in the balloon pushed equally in all directions. When you let the end of the balloon go, the push at that point ceased and the push of the air on the opposite side made the balloon move forward.

As long as the air in the balloon has greater push than the air outside, the balloon is pushed forward. It is the push of the air inside the balloon that pushes the balloon.

The balloon is really a little jet engine.

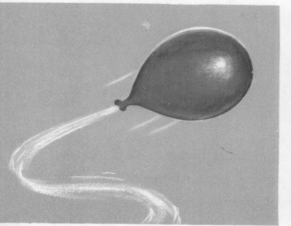 

Big jet engines are not balloons, of course. You would need a huge balloon to hold enough air to push a real airplane. However, there is plenty of air all around the engine. But this air does not have enough push in it.

In a jet plane the air is taken into the engine and changed to give it more push.

The air is changed in two ways.

One part of the jet engine is a strong air pump. This pump pulls in the outside air and squeezes it. To see what squeezing does to air, try this little experiment.

EXPERIMENT

Sprinkle a little dry sand in a heap. Blow up the balloon and then let it empty against the sand. See how much sand is pushed away.

Then collect the sand into a heap again. Blow up the balloon. Let it empty against the sand, but this time squeeze the balloon as it empties.

Do you find that more sand is blown away when the balloon is squeezed? Does air have more push when it is squeezed?

How does the pump of a jet engine help to keep an airplane going when it squeezes air?

Now you know one thing that happens in a jet engine. Air is pulled in and squeezed to give it more push.

Something else is done to the air to give it still more push. The air is heated in a fiercely hot fire.

You have learned what happens to air when it is heated.

When air is heated, it spreads out, or expands. This gives it more push. How does the fire in a jet engine help to keep a jet plane going?

Now you know two important things that happen in a jet engine.

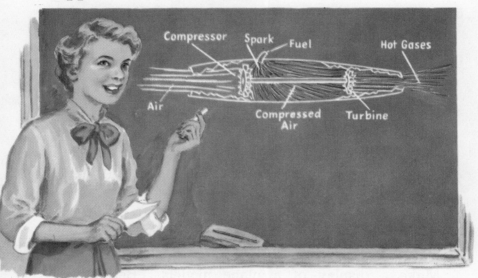

Air is pulled in and squeezed by a pump. Then the air is heated by a fire.

In these two ways the air is changed so that its push becomes very powerful.

The push of the heated air and of the burned gases sends the airplane forward.

Things to Talk About

1. How is an airplane like a bird? How is it different?

2. Have you ever taken an airplane trip? Tell about it.

3. In what ways is air travel better than travel by land or water? In what ways is it not so good?

4. How is a helicopter like an airplane? How is it different?

5. Talk about some ways in which helicopters are especially useful.

6. Have you ever flown a kite? Talk about why a kite can go up in the air.

Things to Do

1. Collect pictures of birds in flight.

2. Watch birds in flight. Try to recognize some kinds of birds by the way they fly.

3. Start an aviation scrapbook. Put in it news and pictures of discoveries and improvements in flying.

4. Make a display of airplane models. Beside each model put a short description of it.

5. Invite someone who builds flying models to show the class how they work.

6. Plan a trip to an airport. Perhaps you can get permission to visit the control tower and the repair shop.

Things to Find Out

1. Find out about these special uses of airplanes: crop-dusting, skywriting, surveying, fighting forest fires. Do you know of other special uses of airplanes?

2. Find out how helicopters are used on airplane carriers.

3. Find out about the tests for a private pilot's license and for a transport pilot's license.

4. Find out about the work of the Montgolfier brothers, Octave Chanute, and Samuel Langley.

5. Find out how an airplane is made to go up and down, to the right and to the left.

6. Find out about the travels of the monarch butterfly and of the golden plover.

7. Find out about air freight.

8. Find out what the CAA is and what its work has to do with aviation.

YOU USE AIR

You use air all the time. You breathe air, you work with air, you play with air, you even ride on air.

Let's find out about some of the ways in which you make use of air.

You play with air. When you bounce a hollow rubber ball, or a football or basketball, you are really bouncing air.

EXPERIMENT

Can you bounce an empty balloon?

Fill it with air and tie it. Now can you bounce it?

Squeeze the balloon, first at one place and then at another. You will see that the part of the balloon you squeezed jumps right back when you let it go. The air pushed it back. We say that air is elastic.

Elastic Air

You ride on elastic air. The air in your bicycle tires is like a springy cushion. It softens the bumps for you.

EXPERIMENT

To see what a difference air makes, ride your bicycle over a short piece of pavement. Then ride over the same place in a pull-cart with solid wheels.

Feel those bumps! What aches you would have if the air in your bicycle tires were not elastic! How do you think it would feel to ride in a fast car without air to cushion the bumps?

Air Presses in All Directions

When you squeezed the air in the balloon, you felt it squeeze right back. You also saw the air push out against the balloon in every other direction, too.

Do you think that the air all around you also presses in all directions? Here is how you can find out.

EXPERIMENT

You will need a drinking glass full right up to the top with water, and a card big enough to cover the glass. It is best to do this experiment over a basin or sink, just in case!

Press the card flat over the full drinking glass. Hold it there and turn the glass over.

Then take your hand away from the card. The card should not fall off. The water should not pour out.

The card was not glued to the glass. Something has to push upward to keep the card in place.

First your hand pushed upward. When you took your hand away, what was there underneath the card? There was air, and only air.

The upward push of the air kept the card and water in place. Air pressed upward.

Now turn the glass sideways. Does the card stay on? It should. What is there to keep the card against the glass? Does air press sideways?

Turn the glass in other directions. Does the card stay on? Does air press in any other directions, too? Could you now say that air does press in all directions?

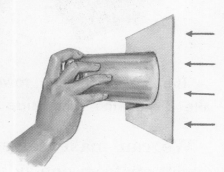

Air is all around you, pressing in all directions. We can use air in many kinds of moving jobs. Here is how you can find out how air is a mover.

Air Is a Mover

EXPERIMENT

Hold a short strip of paper in front of your lips. You know that there is air pressing all around the paper.

If you take away the air from one side, what will the air on the other side do to the paper?

Suck air into your mouth and you will find out.

The paper moves toward your mouth, because the air on the other side of the paper pushes it.

We can make something move by taking away air from one side. The air on the other side pushes it.

That is how a vacuum cleaner picks up dust. There is air all around the dust, pushing from all sides.

If we take away air from one side, the dust will be pushed by air from the other side. In a vacuum cleaner a small electric fan keeps blowing air into a bag.

This leaves a space without air. Other air pushes in, pushing the dust into the bag. The bag is made of cloth or other material with tiny spaces in it. The air can pass through these tiny spaces, but the dirt is kept inside.

When you drink through a soda straw, the air pushes the soda up into the straw. First you have to take out the air in the straw. How do you do that?

Then air pushes the soda. What do you have to do to keep the soda flowing up? Could you drink through a straw if air did not push the soda?

Eye droppers and fountain pens are filled by the push of air. First you squeeze the rubber bulb. What is squeezed out?

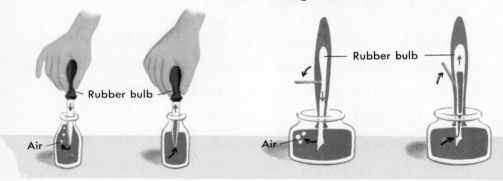

When you let go of the bulb, the sides open out again. The air that was in the bulb is missing. What flows up to take its place? What pushes it up?

Compressed Air

Can you blow hard enough to lift a heavy book? You can if you do it the right way. Place the book on a large balloon or on the bladder of a football or basketball. Blow into the mouthpiece and watch the book rise.

Try it again with two books. See how many books you can lift with your breath.

You were able to lift a heavy load because you squeezed and pressed a lot of air into the balloon. Air that has been pressed into a smaller space is called compressed air. It pushes with more force than the air around you. We use the force of compressed air in all kinds of ways, from bouncing a basketball to stopping a train.

A basketball or a football bounces well because it contains compressed air. So do the tires on bicycles, cars, trucks, and airplanes. The tires can support heavy loads because compressed air has plenty of force. On a bumpy road they smooth out the ride.

A peashooter is a little compressed-air machine. When you blow into it, you push a big breath of air into a little tube. You compress the air. The compressed air pushes the pea with enough force to get you into trouble.

This is another shooter that works by compressed air. It is called a compressed-air drill. The main part is a tube, like the tube of a peashooter. Instead of a pea there is a steel plug called a piston. Compressed air slams the piston down against a pointed tool that digs holes in the pavement. After each slam, compressed air flows against the lower end of the piston and pushes it up for the next slam. The rat-tat-tat that you hear is made by the piston slamming up and down inside the tube, and by the escape of the compressed air.

Compressed-air drill

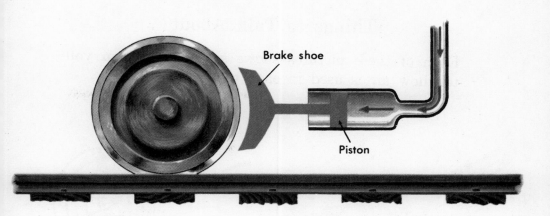

Brake shoe

Piston

This machine is called an air brake. It is used for stopping trains. Like the compressed-air drill, it is a tube with a piston inside. To stop the train, compressed air pushes the piston. The piston forces a curved piece of metal, called a brake shoe, against the wheel. The brake shoe rubs against the wheel and slows it to a stop. The brake in the picture is built to stop one wheel. Most train brakes are built to stop two wheels at once. There are other types as well. In all of them we use thin, invisible air to stop a huge, tremendously heavy train.

Air is surely a useful material for making work easier. Soda straws, fountain pens, fans, brakes, and thousands of other machines and devices make use of the pressure of air.

Things to Talk About

Each of these pictures shows air in use. Can you tell how air is used in each picture?

Things to Do

1. Make a picture chart of things that work by air.

2. Bring to school some toys that work by air. Explain how they work.

3. Is there an air-conditioned building in your community? Take a trip to see the air-conditioning machine. Find out what it does and how it works.

4. Go on a trip to a service station to find out how compressed air is used. Ask to see the machine that compresses the air.

Things to Find Out

1. Find out how a siphon works. Show one to the class and explain it.

2. Find out how a blowgun works and what it is used for.

3. Find out how a submarine is made to go down below the surface of the water.

PLANTS AND MORE PLANTS

How many things made from plants have you used today? Let's look around and see.

Some of your clothing is made from plants.

If your chair is made of wood, you are sitting on part of a plant. The paper in this book was made from parts of plants.

Your breakfast cereal and fruit came from plants.

Actually, you use many hundreds of things made from plants every day.

People everywhere in the world use plants. So do many animals that eat leaves, stems, roots, seeds, and fruits.

Billions of plants are munched, torn out, cut down, and used up every minute of every day. Other billions of plants grow for a season and then die.

Yet the number of plants in the world does not grow less. Most of the world's land is covered with plants. Where do they all come from? How do they keep coming back, year after year?

Ways of Getting More Plants

You know one way we get more plants. We can plant seeds in bare soil and raise more plants with seeds.

But are there other ways that we can get more plants? You can find the answer yourself in an empty lot or at the side of a grassy road.

Find a place where the soil was dug away some time ago. Is the place bare of plants, or have some begun to grow? Perhaps it looks like this.

You can see that there are new plants growing in the bare soil. The grass at the edge is moving in, too. How did the new plants get there? How did the grass move in to the bare soil?

EXPERIMENT

Dig up a small clump of grass. Shake off some of the soil. Then rinse the roots to clear off the rest of the soil.

Do you find separate little plants, or are some of them joined like this?

You will probably find some joined plants. They show one way that grass spreads into bare soil.

A grass plant sends out a little stem. This little stem may be on the surface of the ground or it may be underground.

Then another little grass plant begins to grow from the end of the stem.

After a while this new plant sends out a stem that grows into a new plant. Inch by inch, plant by plant, the grass creeps into bare soil and covers it with a carpet of green.

Many plants creep along, making new plants along the way. Some, like the grass in the picture on page 107, send out underground stems.

Some plants, like the strawberry, send out stems on top of the ground. These stems take root and start another plant.

Strawberry plant

There are plants that send out long roots underground. At places on these roots new stems grow up and new roots grow down. In this way new plants are started.

Bindweed

Walking fern

This plant sends out a long leaf that takes root. It is called a walking fern, because it moves step by step, leaf by leaf.

The Sweet Potato

Spring

Some plants store food in big roots during the summer. In the next summer these roots can sprout new stems and leaves and roots. In this way, just one plant this summer will become many plants next summer.

Sweet potato

The sweet potato is a root of a sweet-potato plant. When sprouts from the root of a sweet-potato plant are planted, each one grows into a plant which makes several more roots.

Fall

Single plants can in this way give rise to a whole cluster of plants that spread out wherever they can. All of these plants get their start from food that was stored up by a single plant the year before.

By trying some planting yourself, you can see a sweet potato begin to make several plants.

Put the sweet potato in a jar of water, with the pointed end down. Pour in enough water to cover the sweet potato halfway up.

Sweet potato

Then put the potato in a warm, dark place. If you have a good sweet potato, new roots will show in about ten days. After the roots form, the vines will begin. Set the plant in the sunlight.

You can get a sweet-potato plant that has many vines.

You can get a new plant because there is a good supply of food stored in the root. Do you think the stored food in the sweet potato can be used by people?

There are some plants that make more plants of their own kind by storing food and spreading out in clusters.

If these roots are planted, each one will send up a new plant that will begin to make new clusters.

Jerusalem artichoke   Ground nut   Tiger lily

Bulbs

There are other plants that store food. They do it in little onionlike growths we call bulbs. You can see for yourself how bulbs grow.

Cut open an onion. The inside is really a group of short, thick leaves very close together.

If you set a whole onion in water, new roots will grow down, and the leaves will grow up.

Have you ever seen onion bulbs begin to grow this way?

112

Can you tell why plants that store food underground can send up spring green before other kinds of plants do?

You have seen how new plants can grow in clusters from a single parent plant. You have also seen how plants can spread out by sending out long roots, stems, or leaves. In these ways a single plant can grow many plants in the soil nearby. Clumps and groups of the same plants may often grow together because they grew from one plant.

Iris

Cattail

People Make More Plants

We can get still more plants, and better ones, by helping the parent clusters to spread apart.

113

We can do this by separating the groups of roots. Each of the little plants is planted in its own bit of soil, instead of being crowded together with the others. In this way the plant can be sure to get the space it needs for good growing.

There are other ways in which people can make many plants out of one plant.

Plants can be cut into several pieces.

If a white potato is cut into several pieces, each piece will grow into a potato plant. Each piece must have an "eye" in it.

Try growing a potato yourself. It is quite easy, especially in the spring.

White potato

Eye

A great many other kinds of plants can be cut into pieces to make more plants. The pieces are sometimes planted in sand to get their roots started. Some are started in water and then planted in good soil. A new plant grows from each piece.

As you can see, we have several ways of getting one plant to grow into many. We can cut apart or separate stems, roots, or bulbs, and each piece grows into a new plant.

You know, too, that plants have their own ways of making many plants out of one, without the help of people. Plants send out spreading roots, stems, or leaves, and then grow clusters of little plants out of a single part of a parent plant.

In all these ways, little plants can grow out of a single parent plant. Many kinds of plants, however, also grow from seeds. In the next unit you can find out how plants make seeds.

Things to Talk About

1. Talk about foods that come from plants. What plant foods have you eaten today?

2. Talk about clothing materials that come from plants. Are any of the clothes you are wearing made of materials that came from plants?

3. Talk about the plants that were used in making the furniture in the room.

4. Talk about what would happen if there were no plants on the earth.

Things to Do

1. Make a chart like the one below. How many things can you add to the chart?

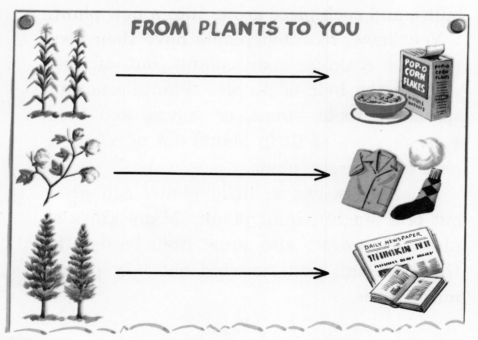

FROM PLANTS TO YOU

2. Visit a greenhouse or a florist shop. Find out which plants were grown from seeds and which plants were grown in other ways.

3. Try growing a new plant from a leaf. Get a leaf from an African violet plant. Place the stem of the leaf in a pot of moist sand. Keep it moist for several weeks. When you can see a new leaf, move the plant to a pot of good soil.

4. Try growing plants from bulbs. Set some paper-white narcissus bulbs in a dish of moist sand or gravel. Put the dish in a dark place until the plants have grown about two inches. Then move the dish into the light. Be sure to keep the sand or gravel moist.

Things to Find Out

1. Find out how bananas are grown. Are the plants grown from seed or are they grown in another way?

2. Tulips are grown from bulbs. Find out where tulip bulbs come from.

3. Find out how we get sugar from plants. These words will help you: sugar cane, sugar beets.

PLANTS AND SEEDS

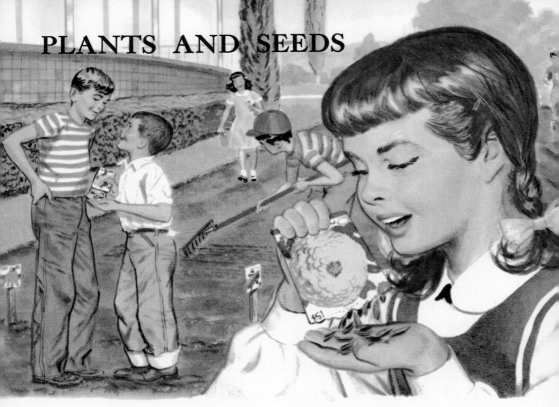

You know that a seed contains a baby plant. If a seed is put into soil, and has sunlight and water and air, the tiny plant in the seed will grow and become a plant like its parents and make more seeds.

A plant has special parts where its seeds are made. These seed-making parts are usually surrounded by lovely, colored petals. Different plants have different-looking petals, but the seed-making parts all do the same kind of work.

In some plants the seed-making parts are tucked inside very tiny flowers. In some plants the parts are big enough to be seen quite well and are inside very large flowers.

Parts of a Flower

In this flower you can see a container shaped like a vase with a long neck. This is called the pistil. The pistils of different flowers look different. But down inside the pistil are little beadlike parts called ovules. Ovules are the beginnings of seeds.

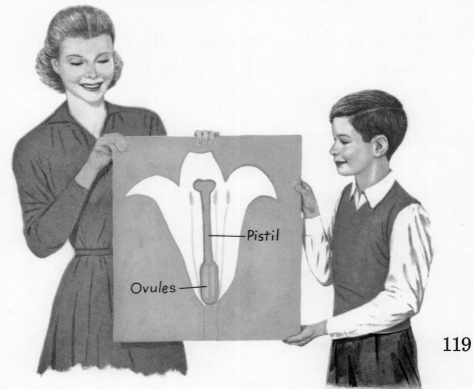

Pistil

Ovules

Most ovules cannot begin to grow and become plants until they get pollen. The pollen is right nearby. It is in the same flower, or in another flower of the same kind. But pollen cannot walk or fly. It must be carried.

How Pollen Is Carried

Some birds and insects carry pollen from flower to flower. Perhaps you have seen hummingbirds flitting about a garden. With their long beaks they sip a sweet liquid called nectar. The nectar is deep inside the flower.

Insects such as bees, butterflies, and moths like to go crawling among the flowers. They, too, sip nectar.

Hummingbirds

Hollyhocks

Forsythia

Spring Azure
butterfly

When a bird or an insect reaches into the flower, it becomes dusted with pollen. When it goes to the next flower, some of the pollen is brushed off onto the pistil. A little tube begins to grow down through the pistil from each pollen grain. The material in the pollen grain then flows downward through this tube and into an ovule.

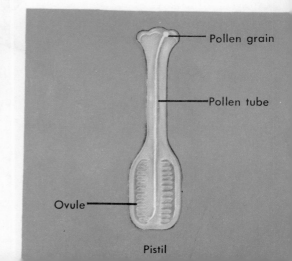

Pollen grain

Pollen tube

Ovule

Pistil

Together, ovules and pollen can change into seeds. The seeds contain baby plants that can grow into big plants.

The colors and sweet smells of flowers are useful to the plant, too. They help to attract insects and birds that carry pollen from flower to flower. Without pollen, most flowers could not make seeds.

Some plants have small flowers, without bright colors or pleasant perfumes. These flowers do not attract insects. Their pollen is usually scattered by the wind.

However, no matter how differently the flowers look or smell, they make seeds in the same way — out of ovules and pollen grains. Then the

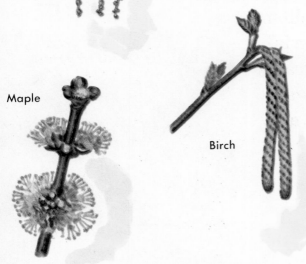

Oak

Maple

Birch

Pine

seeds grow and ripen. The pictures below show how this takes place in some plants we grow for food.

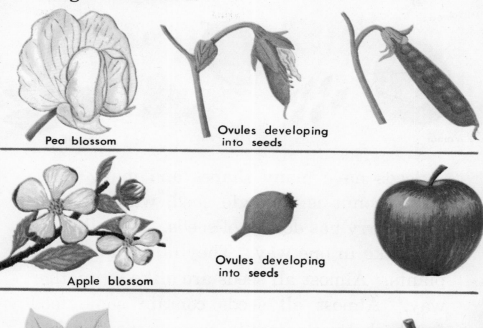

Pea blossom

Ovules developing into seeds

Apple blossom

Ovules developing into seeds

Pumpkin blossom

Ovules developing into seeds

The world is full of plants that make seeds. They have petals of every color in the rainbow. They have lovely shapes and sweet perfumes. People raise them for their beauty and their sweet smell.

What Is in a Seed?

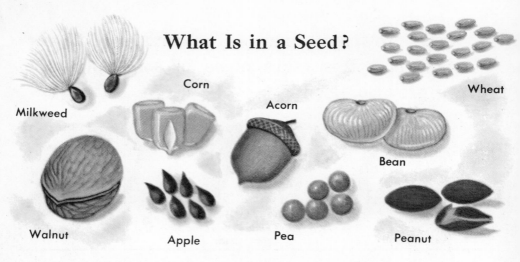

Milkweed Corn Acorn Wheat Bean Walnut Apple Pea Peanut

Seeds have many shapes and many sizes. The coconut is a single seed, while a little strawberry has dozens of seeds. But all seeds are alike in one way. They all contain baby plants. Almost all seeds are alike in another way. Almost all seeds contain some food for the baby plants. In some seeds this food is part of the baby plant and in some it is in another part of the seed. But in almost all seeds there is enough stored food to give the baby plants a start in life.

Bean Peanut Corn Walnut

In some seeds you can easily see the baby plant. It is easy to see the baby plant in a lima bean. A lima bean is a seed of a lima-bean plant. The two halves of the bean are a part of the baby plant. The two halves contain the food that the baby bean plant uses for a while after you plant the seed. The baby plant actually uses part of itself for food. The two halves are pushed out of the ground when the seed sprouts.

Soak some lima beans and then split them open. You can see the baby plant with its two seed halves and its tiny root.

You have eaten lima beans, so you know that they are food for you. Perhaps you did not know that they are used by the baby plant. Here is an experiment that shows that they are used by the baby plant.

EXPERIMENT

Here are the things you will need.

Six lima beans. Three small containers. (Paper drinking cups or ends of milk cartons or flowerpots will do.) Enough sand to fill the containers. A cardboard box big enough to cover the three containers and at least one foot high.

Wet the sand, then put it in the containers. You do this in order to be sure not to "drown" the beans. Now plant two beans in each container. Plant them on edge, with the rounded edge up. This edge should be covered with about one-half inch of sand.

Put all three containers under the cardboard box. Lift the box every day to find out whether the bean plants are growing. At this time add about one tablespoonful of water to each container. In about one week your plants will probably look like this.

Now make three labels — 2 seed halves, 1 seed half, 0 seed halves. Fasten one label to each container.

If the seed coats have not fallen off, carefully remove them.

Do nothing else to the beans in the container labeled "2 seed halves."

Be very careful as you do the next job. You are going to remove one seed half from each of the beans labeled "1 seed half." Hold the plant firmly between your thumb and first finger. Then gently bend back one seed half. You will find that it breaks off easily. Do this to both plants in the container.

Remove both seed halves from the plants in the container labeled "0 seed halves."

Put all containers back under the box. Each day take a quick look. Then cover them again. Each day add a little water.

Soon you will see great differences. All the plants will grow some. The picture shows you how one experiment looked three weeks after the beans had been planted.

Do you know why the beans were kept in the dark? This is so that the only food they have comes from the beans themselves. In the light, beans can make their own food.

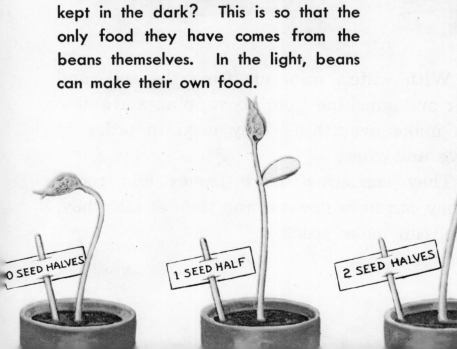

Of course, most beans are planted in the ground. By the time they have used up their food, their leaves and roots have started to grow. By that time they can make their own food.

With water, minerals from the soil, and air and sunshine from above, plants are able to make everything they need in order to live and grow.

They can grow more leaves and roots. They can form flowers, and then at last they, too, can make seeds.

Seeds Travel

Coconut palms

This tiny island is far from the nearest land. Yet it has trees and other green plants growing on it. How did they get there?

Plants have many ways of sending their seeds far and wide.

Some seeds are carried by wind. They have threads or sails or wings which catch the wind.

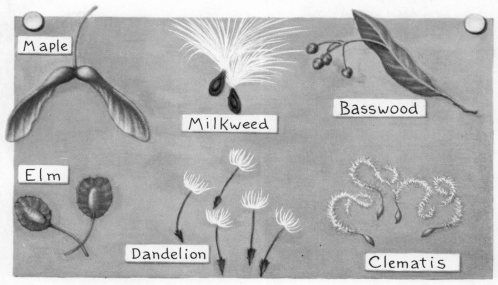

Maple

Milkweed

Basswood

Elm

Dandelion

Clematis

These seeds are carried by the wind.

Red-maple seed

Bladder nut

Some seeds are carried by water. They may drift many miles with the moving water until a wave washes them ashore.

Some seeds are carried by animals. Many of these seeds have little hooks that catch on fur or feathers.

Some seeds have sticky coats that help them cling to the feet of birds and other animals.

Robin

Some seeds even travel inside animals. When a bird eats a cherry or a berry, the pits, which are seeds, stay whole. The hard-covered seeds are passed out of the body with the food wastes.

People, too, spread seeds far and wide. They collect them from grown plants and they plant them in many places.

Sometimes people carry seeds thousands of miles, much farther than the seeds could have traveled by wind or water, or by animals. There were no potatoes in Europe before people brought them from America.

There were no tulips here until the Dutch brought them from Holland.

Many plants have been brought from one place to another. Across land and sea, people share the fruits of the earth.

Things to Talk About

1. Talk about foods made from seeds. How many seed foods can you name?

2. How are some insects useful to plants? How are some plants useful to insects?

3. Tell how all flowers are alike. Describe some ways in which they are not alike.

4. Tell how all seeds are alike. Describe some ways in which they are not alike.

5. Talk about animals that bury seeds. Why do they do this?

Things to Do

1. Go on a trip to a garden or a greenhouse to see different kinds of flowers.

2. Examine a flower with a magnifying glass. Can you find the pistil and the ovules?

3. Examine pollen grains with a microscope.

4. Get different kinds of seeds and mount them on a chart. Next to each kind, put a picture of the plant from which it came.

5. Is birdseed a single kind of seed, or is it a mixture of different kinds? To find out, sprinkle some birdseed on a moist sponge and put the sponge in a shallow dish of water. In a few days the seeds should begin to sprout. Do all the young plants look alike?

132

6. Do seeds need sunlight to start growing? Plan and do an experiment to find out. Radish seeds are good for this experiment because they grow quickly.

Things to Find Out

1. Seed packages are usually marked with a number called "Percentage of Germination." Ask a farmer or a florist what this means and why it is important.

2. Some plants have unusual ways of scattering their seeds. Find out about some of these plants: cat-tail, milkweed, dandelion, clematis, maple, touch-me-not, pansy, violet, witch hazel, mistletoe, burdock, cherry, tumbleweed.

3. Find out about some plants that do not make seeds. Some of these are mushrooms, puffballs, ferns, and mosses.

4. Sometimes a person carries pollen from one flower to another. Find out from a florist how this is done.

INSECTS THAT WORK TOGETHER

Honeybees

Today is apple-blossom day for this busy bee. From blossom to blossom, the bee buzzes along. At each stop she sips nectar and collects some pollen in the little pollen baskets on her legs.

Some of the pollen brushes off on other apple blossoms and gets them started into seed-making. But the flowers are so loaded with pollen that there is plenty of pollen for both the bees and the flowers.

When the bee is loaded with nectar and pollen, she will fly back to the hive. There the nectar will be made into honey and the pollen grains into bee bread.

Bread and honey — this is the food of a bee.

The apple blossoms are far from her hive, yet the bee did not wander about looking for them. She knew where to go.

That morning, a bee scout brought the good news into the hive. Apple blossoms are opening!

The scout even told how far to fly, and in what direction. This is how the bee scout told the news.

First the scout circled around and around a certain number of times. That told the other bees how far to go.

The direction the scout points its body during part of the dance tells the other bees which way to go.

135

Buzzing around the scout, the other bees can smell the sweet, delicate odor of apple blossoms.

Then they know how far to fly, which way to fly, and what to look for.

Off go those bees whose special work is collecting nectar and pollen.

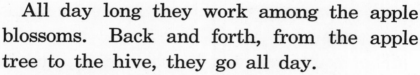

All day long they work among the apple blossoms. Back and forth, from the apple tree to the hive, they go all day.

In the hive the nectar and pollen are made into honey and bee bread. These are stored in little spaces called cells.

Later in the year, and all through the cold winter when there are no flowers to find, there will be bread and honey because the collector bees worked in the summer.

Honeybee cells

Queen bee

Worker bee

Drone

There are many kinds of work to do in a beehive. The bees that buzz over you on a summer day are probably worker bees collecting honey.

Back in the hive other worker bees are feeding and cleaning the baby bees. Some of the baby bees will be workers. Some will be drones. Drones are male bees. One of them may become the father bee of a hive.

Some of the bees are building the six-sided wax cells. Other bees keep the hive clean. There are bees that stand watch at the entrance of the hive. They keep out any strange thing that

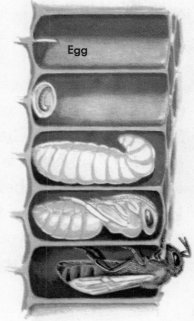
Egg

How a bee grows up

137

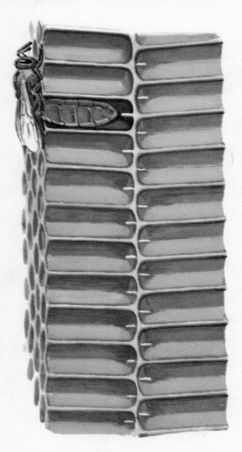
Queen bee laying eggs

dares to come in, even a bee from another hive.

Deep inside the hive, there is the queen bee, who is the mother of all the baby bees. Her work is to lay eggs in cell after cell. She does nothing else but this very important work. Other bee workers feed her, and they keep her and the place around her perfectly clean.

Bees live together and work together. All the bees together make a snug, clean home for themselves. Their young hatch and grow up safely inside the hive. The food that the worker bees gather and store in summer keeps all the bees fed through the winter.

Dividing the work and sharing the food and home seems to work well for bees.

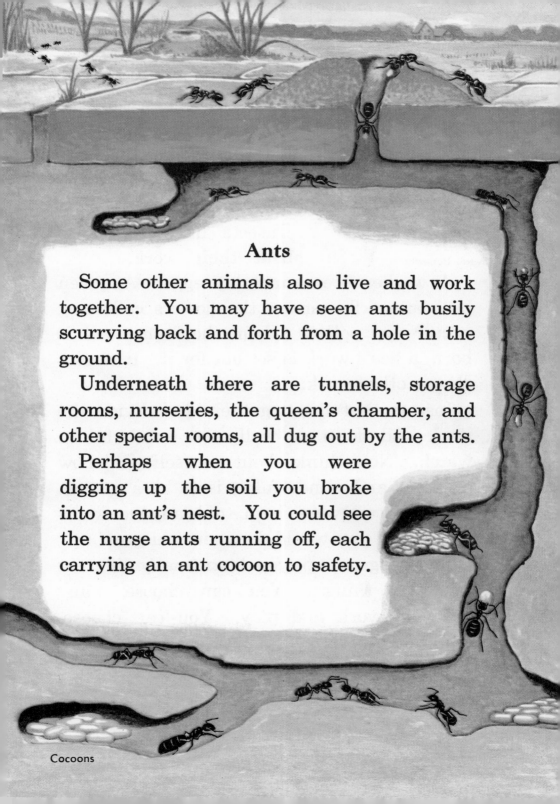

Ants

Some other animals also live and work together. You may have seen ants busily scurrying back and forth from a hole in the ground.

Underneath there are tunnels, storage rooms, nurseries, the queen's chamber, and other special rooms, all dug out by the ants.

Perhaps when you were digging up the soil you broke into an ant's nest. You could see the nurse ants running off, each carrying an ant cocoon to safety.

Cocoons

Tiger swallowtail butterfly

Insects and People

The way these insects work and live together may remind you of people. However, there are some big differences.

Insects have no choice about their work.

A worker bee cannot lay eggs. A queen bee cannot fly among the flowers collecting nectar and pollen. From the moment it is born, a bee's work is set out for it. It cannot choose other work.

Insects that live together, and divide the work and do it so well, are wonderful to watch. Now think about yourself, and how different and wonderful it is to be a person.

When you were born, did anyone know what work you would do when you grew up?

As you grow up, you learn many different kinds of things. You can choose many kinds of work and play. You can choose, and you can change your mind!

Aren't you glad you are a human being?

Things to Talk About

1. Talk about the differences between the way insects live and work together and the way people live and work together.

2. Talk about the advantages of living and working together.

3. Talk about how bees are useful to us.

4. Talk about how a bee scout tells other bees where to find fresh blossoms. Do you know of other ways in which animals communicate with one another?

Things to Do

1. Get a comb of honey. (You can buy combs of honey at some grocery stores.) Cut the comb into small pieces for everyone to examine. Look at the six-sided cells. Smell the pleasant smell. Taste the honey and the wax.

2. Is there a beekeeper in your community? If so, plan a trip to find out about his work.

3. Find an anthill. Sprinkle some sugar nearby and see what the ants do with it.

4. Make a clay or earth model of an ant community like the one shown on page 139.

5. Make a chart or a picture collection of animal homes.

6. Visit a carpenter or a house-builder. Ask him about termites. Perhaps he can show you a piece of wood with a termite nest inside. Find out how new buildings are protected against termites.

Things to Find Out

1. Find out about the different kinds of ants in an anthill and the work that each kind does.

2. Find out how honeybees keep their hives warm in winter and cool in summer.

3. Find out about bumblebees. Do they live together as honeybees do?

4. Find out how paper wasps and mud-dauber wasps build their homes.

5. Find out about other insects that live together. Some of these are leaf-cutting bees, army ants, and termites.

6. Find out about the insects called aphids. Why are they sometimes called ants' cows?

7. Find out how to treat a bee sting.

8. Find out how we can keep ants out of our homes.

9. Find out the meanings of these words: larva, pupa, cocoon, chrysalis.

CLIMATE

The Far North

This is the far north, where the winters are long and the summers are short.

In the winter it is night almost all the time, and in the summer there is daylight almost all the time.

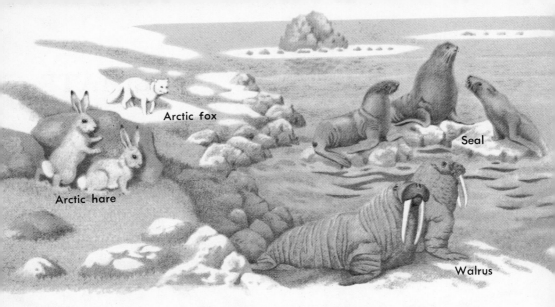

Arctic fox

Seal

Arctic hare

Walrus

At the farthest north point on the earth, the North Pole, the sun sets in September every year and does not rise again until March. Then the sun stays up without setting until it is September again, when it sets for another six months of night. Even as far south as many parts of Alaska the summer days and the winter nights are eighteen to twenty hours long. The winters are very cold in the far north, but although the summers are short it is often very warm in the middle of the summer days.

This is a part of the world where people must work very hard to get food, shelter, and clothing.

The Eskimos have learned how to live in this land of ice and snow. They have learned how to get everything they need from the animals of the cold sea and the frozen land.

Their clothing is made of animal skins and furs. Their food is the meat of these animals. The fuels for light and heat are animal fats and oils. The homes themselves are often made of animals' skins. In a land where the plants are few, the Eskimos have learned how to use animals for almost everything they need.

The Eskimos know how to live well in the cold north. They live in snug, dry homes. They travel in swift sleds and strong, light boats. They make tools and traps and fishing things.

They have time to make toys for the children, to carve ivory, and to have parties and music and dancing. The Eskimos have learned to live happily in the land of the far north.

The Long Cold

Perhaps you have wondered why it is so cold in the far north. Here is one reason why the weather is so very cold.

You know that the heat of the sun warms the earth. The weather is hot when lots of sunlight makes it so. When there is less sunlight, the weather is usually cooler.

In the far north, the winters are long and dark, with no sunlight for months at a time. The sun does not rise at all during the winter months.

There is only the light from the moon and from faraway stars shining on the white snow. People get up, go about their work, eat, and go back to sleep in the same twilight.

There is no sunlight to warm the frozen land and sea and the cold, windy air. No wonder the long winter months are cold!

POLAR BEAR

Short Summer

But there is a strange thing about the far north. In the summer there is plenty of sunlight. The sun does not set at all. It shines and shines for months at a time. You would think that so much sunlight would almost broil the earth. Yet this does not happen. The summers in the far north are short and mostly cool! Only for a month or two is it warm enough for some of the ice and snow to melt, although it is often hot in the middle of the day during the summer.

Is there something different about the sunlight in the far north? Let's find out.

Cold Sunlight

On a summer day in your town the sun shines high in the sky. The sunlight is bright and hot. The shadows are short.

Here is the same place later in the day. The sun is low in the sky. The light is not so bright now in the evening. The buildings cast long shadows. The hot summer day is getting cool.

It is noon on a summer day in the far north, too. But the sun is not high overhead. It looks more like our evening sky. The sun is low down.

Now it is evening of the summer day in the far north. The sun is low in the sky. The sunlight is not bright and hot.

You know that it feels cooler when the sun is low in the sky. In the far north, in the summer, the sun stays low in the sky. Summer there is cooler than summer in the United States.

Why is the sunlight colder when the sun is low in the sky?

You know that when the sun shines from high overhead it gives lots of heat. When it is low in the sky, it gives less heat. How can the same sun give two different amounts of heat? Here is how you can find out.

EXPERIMENT

Fold a sheet of black paper in half. Fasten a smaller piece of black paper to each half, to make a pocket. Place the sheet in the sunlight so that it is raised a little from the table top, as in the picture.

As the picture shows, half of the paper is getting the light straight down on it. We say it is getting vertical light. The word "vertical" means straight up and down. The other half is getting light at a slant.

Now slip a thermometer in each pocket. After a few minutes take the thermometers out and read them. Which part of the paper is warmer?

You will find that the part getting the vertical light is warmer than the part that gets the light at a slant.

Now try the same experiment with a ball. Wrap a piece of black paper around it.

Then hold the ball in the sunlight. Which part gets warmer?

You will find the same thing. The part where the light strikes vertically is warmer than the part where the light strikes at a slant.

The light is the same, but the way it heats each part of the ball is different. The slant of the light makes the difference.

How does the slant make a difference in the climate?

You know that the earth is a ball, too. It receives light from the sun. The sun strikes some parts of the earth vertically. The climate in these parts is very warm.

152

The sunlight strikes other parts of the earth at a slant. These parts are warmed only a little. The sunlight strikes the far north at a slant. The climate is not very warm.

Now you know why summer at the far north is cooler than summer in the United States.

The sunlight strikes the far north at a slant. The ground is heated only a little. But the sunlight is less slanting on the United States. The ground is heated much more.

The same sun shines on both places, but the amount it heats each place is different. The slant makes the difference.

Dark Earth and White Snow

In the experiments you have just done, you used black paper. In one experiment you found that black paper heats up more in vertical light than in slanting light.

In another experiment you wrapped black paper around a ball. Again you found that the ball heats up more in the part where the light strikes vertically.

But why do we use black paper? If you do not know, here is a way to find out.

EXPERIMENT

Get a sheet of black paper and a sheet of white paper. Put both sheets in the sunlight or under a strong electric-light bulb. Place a thermometer under each sheet of paper. Look at the thermometers every minute for five minutes.

Which becomes hotter?

You will find that the black paper becomes hotter.

Black or dark-colored things can become very warm in a strong light.

White or light-colored things are not warmed so much.

Darkness and lightness make a difference in the way something heats up.

Darkness and lightness make a difference in the climate, too.

Dark, cold earth warms up quickly in the sunlight. But white, cold snow does not.

Places that are covered with snow take a longer time to warm up in the spring.

154

This is another reason why the far north is a cold place. It takes a long time for the white snow to be melted by the sunlight. By the time the snow has melted, winter is near again.

Now you know why the climate is cold in the far north.

In the winter it is cold because the sun does not rise at all. There is no sunlight to warm the land, sea, and air.

In the summer the sunlight comes at a slant. Slanting light warms the land, sea, and air only a little. The weather does not get very warm.

White snow does not warm up and melt quickly. This helps keep the weather cold.

For all of these reasons, the far north has a cold climate. We say it is in the Frigid Zone.

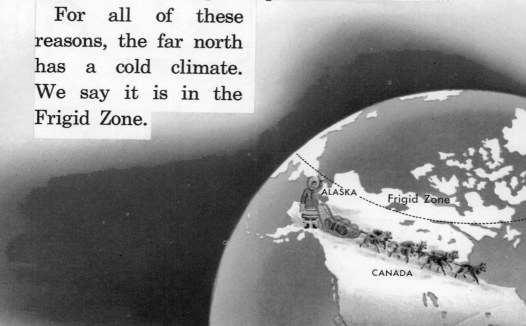

Look at each animal in the pictures. Tell what kind of food each one eats. These animals live in the Frigid Zone.

Tell how each animal protects itself. Which animals run swiftly? Which ones cannot be seen well in the snow? Which ones have strong teeth, claws, sharp hoofs, or horns? Tell how the seal's webbed toes, blubber, and heavy fur help it to live in the icy water. Tell how the Eskimos use each animal.

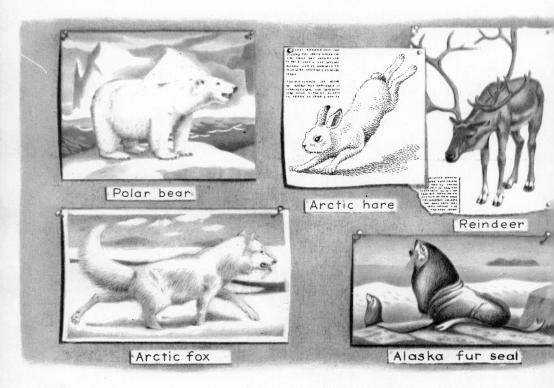

Polar bear

Arctic hare

Reindeer

Arctic fox

Alaska fur seal

Hot Climate

Hot, hot, hot, and then warm, warm, warm! That is the kind of weather you can expect here. The people who live in this village have never known winter. They have never seen snow or ice.

They never need warm clothing.

Their homes are built to keep out the hot sunlight and the steamy rain. They welcome any breeze that may come along.

Here it is always summer — sometimes hot, sometimes warm, but always summer.

Here the land is green all the year round. With plenty of sunlight and plenty of rain, plants grow all the time.

The people who live in a hot climate get almost everything they need from plants.

Their homes are made of plants, their clothing is made of plants, and most of their food comes from plants.

With so much plant life growing all around them, they do not have to work hard for the things they need.

Why Is It Hot?

Why is it so hot here? Your experiment with the folded sheet of black paper told you why.

You found that the sun shone at a slant on part of the paper. That part was heated very little. But the part where the light shone directly from overhead became quite warm.

On this map you can see where the village shown on pages 157 and 158 is located. In this part of the world, the sunlight is more nearly straight down, or vertical, than in other parts of the world.

Every day at noon the sun is high overhead. The rays are vertical (straight down) or almost vertical for many hours each day. The heat piles up.

All year round, sunlight brings summer heat to this part of the world.

The part of the world on which the sunlight falls vertically is called the Torrid Zone.

Parrot

Spider monkey

Can you tell how the color, claws, and beak of the parrot help it to live in this jungle?

The monkey lives in the treetops. Can you tell how its tail and long arms help it to travel through the treetops and how its tail and arms help it to get food?

How is the snake built to get food?

The anteater has sharp claws and a long, sticky tongue. How does this help it to get its food?

Anaconda

Anteater

In-between Climate

Hot weather for part of the year.

Cold weather for part of the year.

If you live in that kind of climate, you probably live in the in-between climate part of the world, the Temperate Zone.

In the in-between zone the rays of sunlight are not so cool and slanting as in the cold zones. Neither are they so nearly vertical and hot as in the hot zones. They are in-between, and so is the climate.

That is the reason why more people live in the Temperate Zone than in any other zone. Here it is not too hot or too cold to live and work comfortably.

In the Temperate Zone, people can raise many different kinds of plants and animals. How does the climate of the Temperate Zone make this possible?

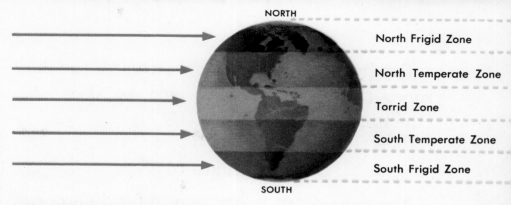

NORTH

North Frigid Zone

North Temperate Zone

Torrid Zone

South Temperate Zone

South Frigid Zone

SOUTH

The Climate Zones

You can see that the greatest slant of the sunlight is at the north and at the south of the globe. These are the cold zones. Between each cold zone and the hot zone there is an in-between zone.

Of course the climate does not suddenly change from one zone to the next. Nor is the climate in one part of a zone exactly like the climate in another part of the zone.

There are many reasons for the different climates. You already know one important reason. You know that the slant of the sunlight makes a difference in the way the earth is heated.

The greatest slant is at the cold zones. These zones have the coldest climate. Then as you go toward the hot zone, the sunlight becomes less and less slanting.

Bit by bit, as you move toward the hot zone, the slant changes, and so does the climate.

Other Climate Makers

The sun's slant is one reason for differences in climate. But it is not the only reason. In the same zone you can find many different climates.

There are cities right in the middle of the hot zone where there is snow and cool weather. In the same zone you can find places where only a little sprinkle of rain falls, perhaps once a year. Yet only a short ride away there are rich farm lands with plenty of rain.

In one place you can go ice skating all winter, while in another part of the same zone it is warm enough to go swimming during the same months.

Yet the slant of the sun may be the same in both places.

As you can see, there must be other causes for the differences in climate all over the world. Let's find out what some of these causes are.

Higher and Colder

In this village in Mexico, the weather is sometimes hot and sometimes even hotter. The direct rays of the sun are fierce and hot all the year round.

165

And here is a high mountaintop only a few miles away from the Mexican village. A thick layer of snow covers the ground. The air is freezing cold. Yet the rays of the sun are nearly vertical all the year round.

What causes the difference? It cannot be the sunlight, since both places have the same vertical rays.

The difference is that the mountaintop is high up in the air, while the village is on low land. Let's see why the weather is cooler high up in the air.

Air Is a Blanket

You know that air is a very good material for preventing the passage of heat. A fur coat keeps you warm because it has lots of air trapped in the fur. It keeps the warmth of your body from escaping.

A fluffy blanket keeps you warm because it has many air spaces tangled in it. It keeps the warmth next to you.

The earth, too, has a blanket of air that keeps it warm. This soft blanket is about six hundred miles thick. It covers the entire earth, and helps to keep it warm.

A thick blanket is warmer than a thin one. The Mexican village has the entire thickness of the blanket of air to cover it and keep it warm.

But the mountaintop is higher up and so it has a thinner blanket above it. That is one reason why the mountaintop is colder.

Mountaintop places are cooler than lowland places because they have a thinner blanket of air. Which place in the picture is at the bottom of the blanket of air? Why is it coolest on the mountaintop?

Sunlight Through Glass

There is another reason why high places are colder. You can find out for yourself with a sheet of black paper.

EXPERIMENT

Place the paper near a closed window, with the sun shining on it. After a few minutes of sunlight, touch the paper.

You will find that it feels warm. There is nothing surprising about that. You know that dark things warm up quickly in the sun.

But now touch the window glass. Does the glass feel warm? Not at all!

The sunlight that heated the paper had to go through the glass first. Yet the sunlight did not heat the glass. But it did heat the paper.

What is the difference between the glass and the paper?

The difference is that glass lets light shine through. We say it is transparent.

Transparent things do not become much warmer when light shines on them.

Try the experiment with other transparent things, such as cellophane.

You will find that these transparent things, too, do not heat up in the sunlight.

Air is very transparent. Sunlight shining through the blanket of air does not heat it.

But the sunlight does heat the earth. Then the earth heats the nearby air. The air near the earth becomes warm in the same way as the air near a hot radiator.

But when you go higher up, you go away from the warm earth. So the air is cooler. With cool air all around, you feel cool, too.

That is why mountain countries often have cool climates. People like to go to the mountains to get away from hot weather.

Because the blanket of air is thinner and cooler up high, transport planes have heating systems. They need to keep the passengers and crew from freezing.

Now you know two important reasons why high places have a cooler climate all the year round.

There is a thinner blanket of air to keep them warm. And they are farther away from the sun-warmed earth that warms the nearby air.

Mountains Make Rain

Mountains can make a big difference in the climate of a land. In many parts of the world they are the cause of a rainy climate. How can mountains cause rain? Let's see.

EXPERIMENT

Hold your hands like this.
Blow against the hand which slopes like the side of a mountain.
You will be able to feel your breath move up and strike the other hand.

MOIST WIND

Mountains

RAIN

UNITED

Pacific Ocean

The same thing happens along mountains near the ocean. Moist winds, full of water vapor from the ocean, blow in across the land.

When a wind strikes a mountain, it moves up along the slope of the mountain. As the moist wind moves up higher and higher, the water vapor meets cooler and cooler air.

You know what happens when water vapor is cooled. It collects into raindrops.

Down comes the rain, flowing down the side of the mountain, watering fields and forests below. Every wind from the sea brings more water vapor.

Mountains that face the winds of the sea make rain for the land.

172

DRY WIND

STATES

Desert

Mountains Make Deserts

On this side of the mountain there is a desert. It is a desert because the mountains make it so.

The mountains chill the sea winds and spill the rain all on the other side of the mountain from the desert. Rarely is there a bit left for the desert side. Once in a great while, a shower of rain falls here.

AUSTRALIA

Desert

Mountains

With the sun beating down and the clouds blocked off, the climate here is hot and dry.

Water Makes Climate

Summers that are not too hot and winters that are not too cold! That is the comfortable kind of climate near large bodies of water.

In the hot summer sunlight the land heats up quickly, but the water does not. Cool breezes from the water blow across the warm land. They mix with the warm air and help to cool it.

In winter, too, water helps to make the climate more comfortable. In winter the land cools off quickly, but the water does not.

The air over the water is warmer than the air over the land. Again there is a mixing of airs, and the land is warmed.

Things to Talk About

1. You have learned about some causes of climate. Which of them are important in causing the climate where you live?

2. Have you been to a place where the climate is different? Tell about it. What are some of the causes of the climate in that place?

3. Choose a place you would like to explore. Find it on a globe. Can you tell what the climate might be at that place? Talk about some preparations you should make before you set off on your exploration.

4. Talk about why people wear dark-colored clothes in cold weather and light-colored clothes in warm weather.

Things to Do

1. Read a book about Eskimo life and make a report on it.

2. Make a model of a home and landscape in the far north. Use salt for snow. You can make an igloo out of clay. Press salt into it while it is soft.

3. Make a model of a home and landscape in a South American jungle.

4. Make a picture chart of some plants and animals used for food in each of the zones.

5. Make a small iceberg by putting a chunk of ice into a deep pan of water. How much of the ice is above water and how much below? Can you tell why a little iceberg may be a big danger to a ship?

Things to Find Out

1. Find out about the explorations of David Livingstone, Robert E. Peary, Roald Amundsen, and Richard E. Byrd.

2. Find out about some animals that migrate great distances from season to season. Some of them are the arctic tern, the blue whale, and the Alaska fur seal.

3. Find out about the laws that regulate the hunting of seals and whales. Why were these laws passed? Why are these animals hunted?

4. Find out what country is sometimes called "Land of the Midnight Sun."

5. Find out ways in which the region around the South Pole is like the region around the North Pole. Find out ways in which it is different.

6. Find out about the climate in which each of the following crops grows best: apples, oranges, cotton, wheat.

Egyptian vulture

Giraffe

Monkey

Eland

Gazelle

WATER, THE STREAM OF LIFE

Far away in Africa, there is a little spot where water comes bubbling out of the ground. It is a water hole, like many others in Africa and in other parts of the world.

Here the animals come to drink. Shy little deer sip delicately. Huge eland with graceful horns bend down to lap noisily with smacking lips. Long-necked giraffes spread their legs wide apart to get close to the cool water.

The animals come to the water hole from miles around. Big animals and little, gentle and fierce, different in many ways, they are all alike in one way. Without water they cannot live.

In a huge city millions of people live and work. Some live in small homes and others in huge apartment houses. They work in offices and factories and stores. Night and day a busy stream of traffic pours through the streets.

Under the city there is another busy stream, flowing steadily. Through huge water mains, water flows in from a faraway reservoir. A crisscross of pipes brings the water to every home and factory, to every part of every street in the city.

Cooking   Fire-fighting   Drinking   Sprinkling

Water for Many Uses   Water from the ↗ Reservoir

Without water there could be no huge city.

In faraway Africa or in your home town, wherever plants and animals live, there must be water for them. Why is water so important to living things?

One reason is that living things are made mostly of water! It may surprise you to find out what a watery person you are. Let's suppose that you weigh seventy pounds. About forty-five pounds of that weight is water. Without water you would weigh less than thirty pounds.

You, other people, dogs, elephants, fish, and other animals are mostly water.

Water in Plants

Plants have even more water in them than animals do. When you buy a ten-pound bag of potatoes, you get about eight pounds of water and two pounds of other materials. A ten-pound watermelon is even more watery. More than nine pounds of the watermelon is water.

Here is a way of seeing for yourself that plants have a great deal of water in them.

EXPERIMENT

Squeeze the juice out of an orange. Let the juice stand for a while and then look at it.

Almost every single drop of the clear liquid is water. A large part of the yellow material at the bottom is water, too.

Pour the juice into a wide dish and let it stand in a warm place. Let all the water evaporate from the juice.

See what a very little bit of material is left. That is about all the solid material inside an orange.

The part of the juice that evaporated was water.

You can find dried plants and see how much of the original plant is left after drying.

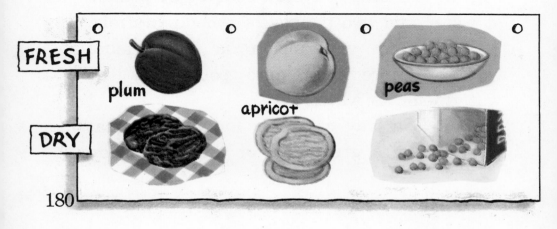

FRESH   plum   apricot   peas

DRY

Water in Meat

Animals, too, have a great deal of water in them. Perhaps you have found this out yourself. When you carry a package of fresh meat home from the butcher, the paper sometimes becomes soaking wet.

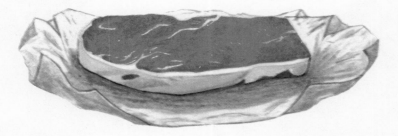

The wetness is mostly water, as you can see by doing this experiment.

EXPERIMENT

Get a small slice of fresh meat and place it between two flat dishes.

Then put this "meat sandwich" in a larger dish or tray, tipped up at a slant.

Rest something heavy on the top dish to press down on the meat.

Soon you will see a liquid oozing out of the meat. Collect the liquid in a glass and let it stand.

You will see it begin to settle, like the orange juice. The clear liquid is almost entirely water.

The darker material at the bottom also has a great deal of water in it.

Now pour all the liquid into a flat dish and put it in a warm place.

Let all the water evaporate. See what a very little bit of material is left.

Would you say that there is a great deal of water in meat?

Now you know one reason why plants and animals cannot live without water. They need it because a large part of every living thing is water.

How Animals and Plants Lose Water

As living things grow, a large part of that growth is water. However, you have to drink more water than you need just for growing. In your food and drink you take in more than four pounds of water every day.

Do you gain four pounds every day? Of course not! Even one pound a week is an enormous amount to gain. What happens to the rest of the water?

Some of this waste water is passed out of your body, when you go to the toilet, in the liquid wastes which are called urine.

Sweat

Some water evaporates from your skin when you perspire. Some water is passed out in your breath.

Breath

You have probably seen the water in your breath, on a cold day. But even when you do not see it happen, you breathe out water. Here is a way of seeing it happen right now.

EXPERIMENT

Hold a mirror near your mouth or nose. Breathe on it. See the mirror become cloudy.

Touch the mirror and feel how wet it is. This wetness is a thin film of water.

The water vapor in your breath was cooled by the cool mirror and gathered into tiny drops of liquid water.

In every breath you give off water into the air.

Now do you know why air in a crowded room often feels damp and sticky?

You breathe out water all the time. So do all animals that breathe.

Do plants lose water into the air, too? Here is a way of finding out.

EXPERIMENT

Get a potted plant and wrap the pot and soil with aluminum foil. Wrap the foil around the stem tightly. Cover the plant with a large glass jar.

Begonia

Wrap another pot that has soil but no plant. Cover this pot with a jar, too.

In a short while look at the jars. You will find that the jar with the plant has a film of water along its sides.

How can you tell that the water came from the plant and not from the soil or the air?

Plants lose water into the air all the time. So do animals. If plants and animals do not get as much water as they lose, they dry up and die.

Without water there can be no life.

Cells

You know now that living things have a great deal of water in them. You know, too, that as long as they live they keep on taking in water. This replaces the water they lose into the air.

Why must they have so much water in them? What work does water do that makes it so important? How is water used by you and all other living things?

People wondered about these questions for thousands and thousands of years. But it was impossible to find the answers just by looking with their eyes.

Eyes cannot see closely enough. To find our answers, we must see into the tiny, tiny parts of living things. To see as closely as that, we must use a microscope.

The first microscope was invented about 350 years ago. Of course, scientists improved the microscope and today we have very good ones. With a modern microscope we can look much more closely than with our eyes alone.

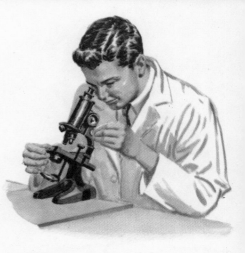

With a microscope, tiny things are made to appear much larger than they really are.

With a microscope we can look right into tiny parts of living things. We can see how many of the parts are made and how they work.

Perhaps you have a microscope in your school. Or perhaps you have a strong magnifying glass that makes things appear larger. Let's look at a piece of living thing with your microscope or magnifying glass.

An onion is a living thing. Take a slice of onion and separate the layers. Find the thin sheet, like tissue paper, attached to each layer of onion.

Put this thin sheet on a piece of flat glass.

Hold it in a strong light and look at it with your microscope or strong magnifying glass. What do you see?

Here is a picture of a piece of onion seen through a microscope. The microscope makes it seem many times larger.

The onion seems to be made of rows of little bricks!

If we use a still stronger microscope, a single one of these bricks looks like this.

Onion-skin cells

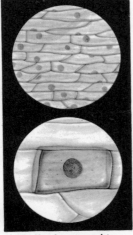

Cell of onion skin

It does have a shape like a brick or a shoe box. It is called a cell.

A little piece of onion as big as this "o" is made of hundreds of cells.

Different Kinds of Cells

Now let's look at another part of an onion. Here is a bit of the green leaf, seen under a microscope. Again we can see cells, but these cells have a different shape.

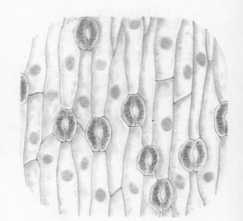

And here is a piece of the root, seen under a microscope. The root was first dipped in a dye to make the parts show clearly. Cells again!

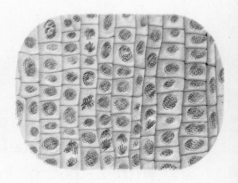

Are animals made of cells, too? Here is what a bit of human skin looks like. The cells are there, even though they are not shaped like bricks.

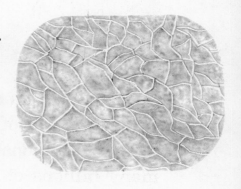

Here is some human
muscle. The cells are
long and thin.

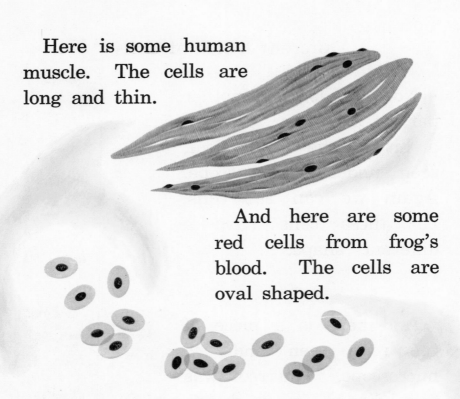

And here are some
red cells from frog's
blood. The cells are
oval shaped.

Here is a bit of lining from
a person's cheek, scraped off
with a toothpick.

Cells, cells, and more cells! Every living
thing is made of cells. A blade of grass is
made of millions of cells. You are made of
many billions of cells.

How Water Is Used by Cells

This brings us to the question that started us hunting for cells. The question was, "How is water used by your body and by all living things?"

We find the answer in cells.

To stay alive and grow, a cell must receive food and other materials from the outside. And water is necessary in bringing food and other materials to a cell.

Every cell is a kind of box, with soft material inside and a somewhat harder cover outside.

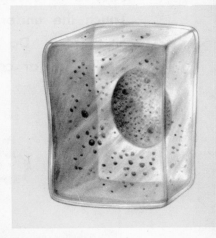

The cover goes all the way around the cell. There are no special openings in it. Yet food must get into it. How can the food get into the cell?

You can find the answer by doing a little experiment. You will need a piece of paper towel, a teaspoonful of sugar, and a little water. You will also need a clean pair of hands.

EXPERIMENT

Fold the paper into a little cone, as in the picture.

Notice that there is no opening in the bottom of the cone.

Pour a little sugar into the cone.

Touch the underside of the cone and then taste your fingers. Do you taste any sugar? Of course not. Dry sugar cannot pass through paper.

Now pour a little water into the paper cone. As the water soaks through, catch a few drops and taste them.

Do they taste sweet? Can sugar and water pass through the paper? You find that they can.

The same thing happens with a cell. Dry things cannot pass through the covering of the cell. But when they are dissolved in water, many things can pass through.

Dissolved food passes through the cell covering easily. Dissolved air also passes through easily.

Anything can pass through, if it is dissolved in water.

Everywhere in your body, water carries the precious materials that your cells need. Your blood is mostly water. As your blood flows through every part of you, it brings a steady supply of materials that the cells need and carries away the things it no longer needs.

You have billions of cells of many kinds, and they need many different kinds of materials.

Yet water can carry them all, because water is a marvelous dissolver. Water can dissolve more different kinds of materials than any other liquid.

Water is the great carrier in living things. Water is the stream of life.

Things to Talk About

1. Talk about how a plant looks when it does not get enough water.

2. Tell why you feel thirsty more often on a hot day than on a cold day. Tell why you feel thirsty after you have been playing hard.

3. Talk about why you can see the water in your breath on a cold day.

4. What are some substances that dissolve easily in water? What are some substances that do not dissolve easily?

Things to Do

1. Make a picture chart of fresh and dried foods. A few of these foods are shown in the picture at the bottom of page 180.

2. Cut an apple or a large peach into slices. Weigh the slices. Heat them in a warm oven for a few hours to make the water in them evaporate. Then weigh them again. How much water has been lost? Try the experiment with other foods. Keep a record of your results.

3. You can make a low-power microscope out of a drop of water. First put a small piece of clear cellophane on a newspaper. Then put a drop of water on the cellophane. See how it seems to enlarge the printing on the newspaper. You can examine other flat things with your water-drop magnifier.

4. Dig up a dandelion and some grass. Which plant has longer roots? Tell why a dandelion plant can stay green during a dry summer.

Things to Find Out

1. Some plants, such as mistletoe and Spanish moss, do not send roots into the soil. Find out how they get water.

2. Many desert plants and animals have special ways of saving water inside them. Find out about some of these special ways.

3. Does your community have a water supply system? Find out how much water is used in a day. About how much does one person use?

4. Find out how powdered milk is made. What are some special uses of powdered milk?

5. Find out why people sometimes eat salt tablets when they are perspiring a great deal.

6. On the underside of a leaf there are cells that control the escape of water vapor from the leaf. (There is a picture of some of these cells at the top of page 189.) Find out how these cells work.

HIGH WATER — LOW WATER

Rice fields in China

Going up, going down, the world's water keeps traveling all the time. The heat of the sun lifts it high up into the air. The cooling of the air makes it fall again.

Water falls to the earth as rain or snow, sleet or hail, but its journeys are not over. It may travel many thousands of miles. It may flow through many strange and secret places before the sun's heat reaches it again.

Let's follow the water on its far travels. What happens after it falls to the earth?

We can't go sailing down the rivers of the world, or go digging underground with the little moles. We can do something, though. We can see some parts of the journey in a little homemade piece of the world.

Water on the Earth

We can see what happens to water that falls on the earth. All we will need is an empty aquarium and some dry sand and soil.

EXPERIMENT

Mix the sand and soil (three fourths sand and one fourth soil), and pack it in a slant against one side of the aquarium. This will be a little slanting hill on which rain can fall.

The rain itself will come from a sprinkling can, or from a milk container with several holes punched in the bottom.

Let the rain fall on the top of the hill and see what happens.

Some of the water streams down along the surface of the hill. Watch it form a puddle at the base of the hill.

See the soil begin to darken under the surface! Some of the water is soaking down into the soil.

When rain falls down from the clouds, it keeps on going down. Some of it flows down along the surface and into streams. Some of it seeps straight down into the earth.

Water Underground

What happens to the water that soaks into the ground?

EXPERIMENT

If you keep on sprinkling your little hill, you will see that more and more of the soil becomes dark, as the water soaks down from the top.

After a while it will soak all the way down to the bottom of the aquarium. That is as far as it will go.

Why does the water stop at the bottom?

You know, of course! The bottom of the aquarium is made of glass or stone.

Porous and Nonporous

Water can soak through many materials. It cannot soak through some materials. There are plenty of little spaces in between the particles of sand and soil. Water can go through them. We say that sand and soil are porous.

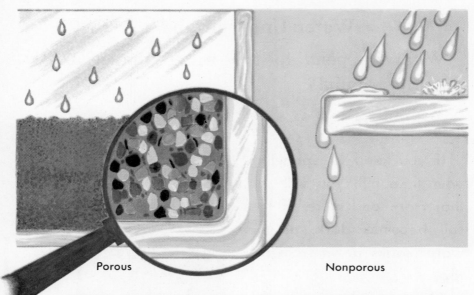

Porous

Nonporous

There are no holes or spaces big enough to let water through the glass. We say that glass is nonporous.

Many kinds of stone are nonporous. The bottom of the aquarium is made of glass or nonporous stone. The water does not go through. It piles up.

When rain water soaks into the earth, it seeps down through the porous sand and soil. It can even seep through some kinds of rock that are porous.

When rain water reaches nonporous rock, it stops. When more water seeps down, it piles up on top of the water already there.

There is underground water almost everywhere in the world. In places where there is a lot of rainfall, the underground water is near the surface. It is also near the surface where the nonporous rock is close to the surface and rain water cannot seep far down.

In other places the underground water is deeper down. That usually happens when the nonporous rock is deep down, too.

The top of the underground water is called the water table. Here you see a well digger drilling to reach the water table.

Porous

Water table

Nonporous rock

Digging for Water

You may like to try digging for water yourself. You can do it quite easily in your little piece of the world, the aquarium.

EXPERIMENT

Pour in enough sand to make a flat layer about eight inches deep.

Then pour in water and let it soak down until the layer of water has piled up about six inches deep.

We call the top line of the water in the soil the water table.

Now let's dig for water. With a spoon, dig a hole in the sand until you reach water. Dig a little more and you will have a little pool or water hole.

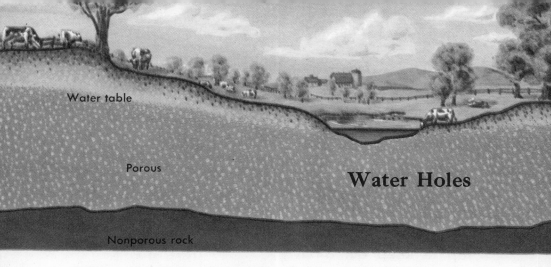

Water table

Porous

Water Holes

Nonporous rock

Many real water holes are places like the one in this picture where underground water is close to the surface. Have you ever seen a water hole in a field or in the woods?

Wells

Now let's make a better water hole than we made before.

EXPERIMENT

Get an empty tin can with its top and bottom cut out. Work the can into the sand until the top of the can is an inch or two above the sand.

Then scoop out the sand inside.

As you scoop, you will see water coming up to take the place of the sand. When you have dug all the way down, the can will have water in it. You will see that the water is at the same height as the underground water in the aquarium.

Why is this a better sort of water hole? Can sand crumble in from the sides? Can a deeper hole be dug this way? Can a cover be built over the top to keep out dirt?

This sort of water hole can be found by the millions all over the world. It is called a well.

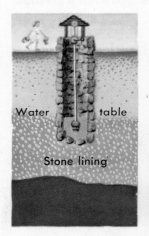
Water table
Stone lining

Brick lining

Tile lining

Real wells are lined with stones, bricks, or tile pipes. Very deep wells are lined with steel pipe. There are many types of wells, but they are all the same in one way.

All of them are holes dug down to reach into the underground water.

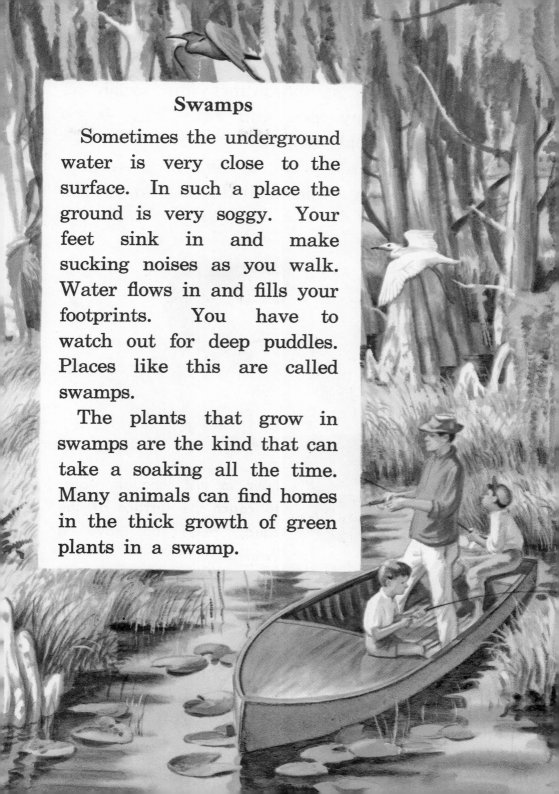

Swamps

Sometimes the underground water is very close to the surface. In such a place the ground is very soggy. Your feet sink in and make sucking noises as you walk. Water flows in and fills your footprints. You have to watch out for deep puddles. Places like this are called swamps.

The plants that grow in swamps are the kind that can take a soaking all the time. Many animals can find homes in the thick growth of green plants in a swamp.

Insects that like water are plentiful here. As you slap at mosquitoes and brush off clouds of tiny flies, you say, "This is no place for people to live!"

You may not want to live in a swamp, but you can build a little swamp in the aquarium.

EXPERIMENT

Pour in just enough water to reach the surface of the sand, and you have a swamp.

Of course our little aquarium swamp is very different from the real kind. To make it more real, you would need to put in a lot of swamp plants and insects.

Draining a Swamp

A swamp is too soggy and mucky for farming. The underground water is too high. If some of the underground water is drained off to make the water table lower, the swamp can be changed to good farm land.

Let's try lowering the water table in your little swamp in the aquarium.

EXPERIMENT

You will need a rubber tube two feet or more in length, a spoon, and a basin.

First scoop out a hole at one end of the swamp.

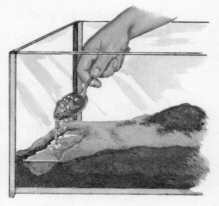

Fill the tube with water by holding one end of the tube under the faucet until water begins to come out of the other end. Then pinch both ends with your fingers to keep the water from flowing out.

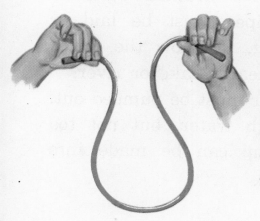

Still pinching, put one end into the hole you scooped in the swamp.

Put the other end of the tube into the basin, which is lower than the aquarium. Watch the water begin to flow into the basin. The first water that flows out is from the tube itself. We put it in to start the flow of water.

You will see that the water keeps on dripping. From where is it coming? Watch the level of the water in the swamp. What is happening?

Real swamps are not drained quite so easily, of course. Pipes must be laid or trenches must be dug, to allow the water to flow down into a nearby lake or river.

Sometimes the water must be pumped out. By letting out enough water, but not too much, a soggy swamp can be made into useful farm land.

Lakes

In a swamp the underground water is very close to the surface, or even slightly above it. Sometimes the water is several feet or more above the land. Then you have a lake.

Water table

EXPERIMENT

You can make a little lake in your aquarium. Just dig out a large hole in the sand near one side of the aquarium. Then watch the water seep in.

Look through the side of the aquarium and you will see that the water in the lake is at the same height as the underground water in the soil.

Deserts

What a difference a few feet can make! When the underground water is very close to the surface, the land is too wet and swampy for most kinds of farming.

When the water is a few feet below the surface, the land is good for farming.

What kind of land would you have if the water were very far below the surface? You would usually have a desert.

Water table

Porous

Nonporous rock

In a desert the soil is dry and sandy. The underground water is too far down to be of use to most plants. Only a few kinds of plants can grow in the desert. Some have long roots or special ways of saving water in their thick, spongy stems. Some desert plants grow just during the rainy season. Only their seeds live through the long dry periods. Others stop growing during dry weather and start growing again when rain comes.

Yet, even in the desert the water is there, deep underground. Enough can be pumped up to supply people and cattle with drinking water. There may be enough to grow rich fields of crops.

With enough power, water can be pumped up to the surface. And with enough water, many deserts can be changed into good farm land. Science can help give the world more farm land. It can help make more farms in the desert by helping to develop low-cost power for pumping water.

Water table

Porous

Land from Under the Sea

How would you like to work on a farm at the bottom of the sea? Many thousands of people do, and not one of them wears a diver's suit. They work on land that is really sea bottom, except that the sea is no longer there.

The land is below sea level, yet people work on it, live on it, and travel on it.

There are many places in the world where sea-bottom land has been changed to dry land. Perhaps the best known of these places is in Holland.

A good part of Holland was once land under a shallow sea. This land was good soil that could feed many thousands of people. This soil was brought down from inland by rivers that flow to the sea. Salt water from the North Sea flowed in and out over this land as the tides changed.

The people of Holland wanted more food than just the fish they could catch in this huge, shallow sea. They set to work at making new land out of the sea bottom.

They built long walls of earth and stone. These walls, called dikes, kept out the water of the North Sea.

The water on the other side of the dikes was pumped out by huge pumps. In the early days these pumps were run by windmills. In modern times they are run by engines and motors. Pumping away, night and day, year after year, they have added hundreds of square miles to Holland. Still today they continue to add good, rich fields for Holland's fine bulb and dairy farms.

A Model Dike

You can build a model dike, with the sea on one side and farms and houses on the other. You will need an aquarium, or a baking dish or a refrigerator dish. The land and the dike can be made of sand, soil, or modeling clay.

Modeling clay is best because it is nonporous. Water will not seep through it.

If you use sand or soil, pack it tightly so that as little water as possible will seep through. To make the water look more real, add a few drops of blue ink, to give it a bluish color.

The trees on the side of the dike can be made of green sponge rubber or plastic cut to shape, with twigs or matches for trunks. Be sure to place your farms below sea level. That is how they really are.

High or Low Makes a Difference

We don't often think about water, except when we are thirsty or about to take a bath. Most of us don't think about the water table at all. But now you know what a difference it makes to everyone.

Is the water table very far down in your part of the country? If it is, you probably live in a place almost dry enough to be desert. Every drop of water is precious in such places, and farming can be carried on only by irrigation.

Is the water table very close to the ground or a little above it? If it is, you don't live here at all, because the ground is too soft and mucky to live on or to farm.

Is the water table high up in the soil? If it is, there is probably plenty of water for people's needs and for the farmer's crops.

Perhaps the water table is way up above the land, as in the sea-bottom land of Holland or the river-bottom land along the Mississippi River. Then you need pumps and dikes to make the land fit for use.

Everywhere, in every land, the water table is somewhere to be found. Where it is, and how deep it is, makes a world of difference to the plants and animals that depend upon it.

Things to Talk About

1. Talk about what happens to the rain water that runs off the roof of your house. What happens to the rain water in the streets?

2. Are there any lakes, ponds, rivers, or brooks in your community? Which of these waters have you visited? Tell about them.

3. Would you expect to find a swamp at the top of a hill or at the bottom? Tell why.

4. Have you ever visited a place where the water table is very high or very low? Tell about it.

5. Talk about what would happen if the water table in your community rose ten feet. Talk about what would happen if it fell ten feet.

Things to Do

1. Here is a way of seeing water spread through a porous material. Color a spoonful of water with some red ink. Touch the corner of a lump of sugar to the colored water. Watch what happens. Can you explain why the soil near a lake is always damp?

2. Which kind of rain is better for a farm — a very heavy rain for half an hour or a light rain for half a day? Perhaps you can plan an experiment to find out. Use two slanting boards with soil on each. What will you use for rain?

3. Is there a well driller in your community? Plan a trip to find out about his work. Prepare some questions to ask him.

4. The pipes that are used to drain swamps are called drainage tiles. Ask a building-supply man to show you one of these tiles. Find out from him how they work.

5. Collect or draw pictures of water in the ground and on the surface. Include pictures of lakes, swamps, wells, springs, and water holes.

Things to Find Out

1. Find out about how much rain falls in your community in a year. Which is the rainiest month? Which month has the least rain?

2. Find out about artesian wells. Are there any in your community?

3. Find out how rice is grown. Find out how cranberries are grown. How are the places where rice and cranberries are grown alike? How are they different?

4. Find out what an oasis is.

5. Find out what quicksand is. Why is it dangerous?

6. Find out the meanings of these words: topsoil, subsoil, bedrock.

PURE DRINKING WATER

Have a drink of water!

Which glass would you take? Certainly not the muddy one. It doesn't look good, and you can be fairly sure that it doesn't taste good, either.

What about the glass of clear, sparkling water? It looks good and it probably tastes good. Yet you cannot be sure.

The look and taste of water cannot tell you whether it is fit to drink. You need to know if there are disease germs in the water.

Filtering Water

Disease germs are much too tiny to see without a microscope. A hundred thousand germs of average size could be lined up in the space between these two dots: •   • You cannot taste them in a glass of water. Yet they can be very harmful. One sip of water containing typhoid germs is enough to give a person a violent case of typhoid fever.

How do the germs get into the water?

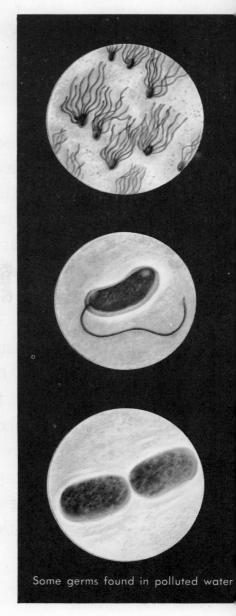

Some germs found in polluted water

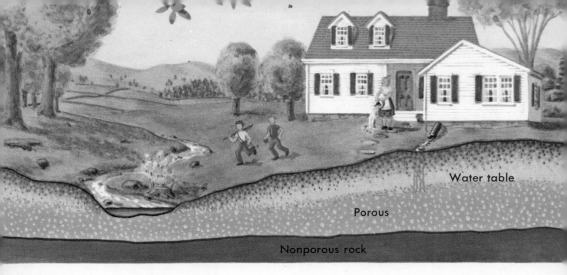

Water table

Porous

Nonporous rock

Can you see how water seeping down from the surface could carry germs into the brook and pollute the water?

The germs might seep into a well, too, even though it is lined with stones. The water in wells and springs should be tested from time to time to make sure that it is not polluted. Your board of health will make these tests free of charge.

Water can be polluted in other ways. Perhaps some town runs its sewage pipes right into a stream that flows into a river nearby. There may be a factory which empties its waste materials and chemicals into a flowing stream. Far up the river, someone may decide that the town water is just the thing for swimming. That is why most communities have water departments. Inspectors see that the water is kept pure.

Most communities also have something else. They have water-purification systems.

To make water fit to drink, the disease germs must be removed or killed. At the same time the water must be cleared of sand, soil, tiny plants, and other things that make it cloudy or give it a bad taste. Let's see how this is done.

Water can be cleared by letting it flow slowly through layers of sand and gravel. These materials act like strainers or filters, which let the water filter through but hold back most of the solid materials. However, some of the smaller disease germs can get through a filter of even the finest sand.

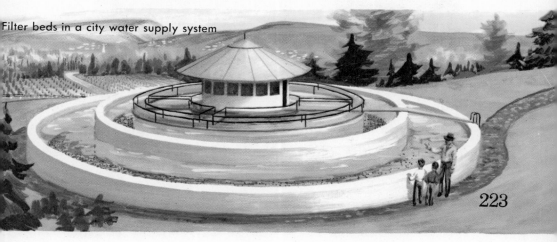

Filter beds in a city water supply system

EXPERIMENT

You can make a little filter in a few minutes. You will need a milk carton, some clean sand, some clean gravel, a drinking glass, and some muddy water. Gravel is a mixture of small stones and pebbles.

Punch many little holes in the bottom of the carton. Then pour in about three inches of gravel. On top of the gravel add three inches of sand. Rest the carton on the drinking glass and your filter is ready for business.

Pour muddy water on top of the sand. Let it filter through.

After a while, filtered water will begin to drip through into the glass. You will see that it is clear.

Killing Germs in Water

Even though water that has been filtered through sand and gravel is clear, it may still contain harmful germs. These germs cannot be seen just by looking at the water.

The germs that get through the sand filter are very tiny, but some of them may be disease germs. To make the water fit for drinking, the germs must be killed.

This is usually done by adding to the water small amounts of a chemical called chlorine. The small amounts of chlorine in the water are harmless for people to drink.

If you have a microscope at school, you can see how chlorine kills germs.

EXPERIMENT

Get some stagnant water from a quiet pool or ditch or from a vase in which flowers have been standing for several days. Stagnant water is water that has been standing for a long time.

This water is almost sure to have some tiny animals swimming around in it. These tiny animals can be seen with a microscope. They are bigger than germs but are otherwise very much like germs.

You will also need a few drops of bleaching water. This is used for bleaching white clothing after it is washed. Bleaching water contains chlorine.

Put a drop of the stagnant water on the microscope slide. Look through the microscope to see whether you have tiny animals swimming around.

If you have these little animals, put a tiny bit of bleaching water on the drop of stagnant water.

You can see that the chlorine kills these little animals very quickly. It also kills any disease germs that may be in the water. The tiny dead germs are completely harmless.

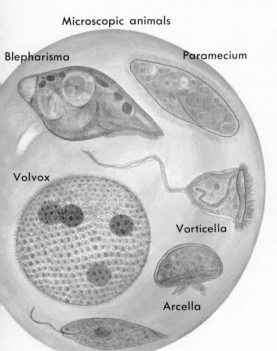

Microscopic animals

Blepharisma

Paramecium

Volvox

Vorticella

Arcella

Euglena

Putting Air in Water

In some water systems the water is sprayed through the air. This helps oxygen from the air to mix with the water, giving it a fresh, clean taste.

Aeration fountains

Perhaps you can take a trip to the water works nearest your school. Here are some questions to answer after your trip.

1. Where does the water come from?
2. Where is it stored?
3. When the water enters the reservoir, is it entirely clear?
4. Are there trees along the banks of the reservoir? How do they help to keep the water clear?
5. If the water is not entirely clear, how are the tiny bits of sand, soil, and plants removed?
6. How is the water tested to be sure that it is pure and fit to drink?

Things to Talk About

1. You have found out that sand and gravel are used for filtering water. Can you tell why water from a deep well is usually safer than water from a shallow well?

2. Talk about safety rules for drinking water on camping trips.

3. Tell why we can help to make water safe to drink by boiling it.

4. Talk about why water that has just been poured tastes better than water that has been standing for some time.

Things to Do

1. Ask the school custodian to show you the pipe that brings water into your school. Trace the flow of water up to a faucet on the first floor.

2. Take apart an old faucet to see how it works.

3. Invite a plumber to visit your class. Prepare a list of questions to ask him.

4. Collect pictures showing some of the uses of water.

5. Most drinking water contains some dissolved minerals. Put a few drops of water from a faucet on a clean piece of glass. Let the water evaporate. You may see a few whitish or grayish stains on the glass when the water has evaporated.

Things to Find Out

1. Find out how your community was supplied with water one hundred years ago.

2. Find out about the water supply system in your community today.

3. Find out about hard water and soft water. Which kind is better for most uses? Which kind does your community have?

4. Find out what happens to the waste water from kitchens and bathrooms in your community.

5. Find out what diseases can be passed along through water. A doctor or a public health officer can tell you.

6. Find out how sea water can be made fit to drink.

7. Is there a factory in your community? Find out what it does with its waste materials.

8. Find out what distilled water is. How is it different from ordinary pure drinking water?

SEASONS

North Temperate Zone

South Temperate Zone

Happy New Year! A skating party in the winter is a fine way to start the new year.

Happy New Year! A summer swimming party is a fine way to start the new year, too.

Winter in one zone, summer in another. Both are temperate zones and yet the seasons are opposite. Let's see how this can be.

The Earth's Orbit

You know that the earth is round and that it turns steadily. Each turn brings night and day on the earth.

The earth moves in another way, too. As it turns, it also travels around the sun. The earth's path around the sun is called the earth's orbit.

The earth travels in the same orbit year after year. Each trip around its orbit takes a whole year, through summer, fall, winter, spring.

Earth

Sun

The two motions of the earth go on at the same time. As the earth travels around the sun, it also turns through day and night.

One year to go around

The earth makes $365\frac{1}{4}$ turns during one trip around its orbit. There are $365\frac{1}{4}$ days and nights in a year. How many trips around the sun have you made since you were born?

The Earth's Axis

Now let's see how it can be winter and summer on the earth at the same time.

Earth's axis

North Temperate Zone

South Temperate Zone

The picture at the bottom of page 232 shows how the sun's rays shine on the earth in late December. You can see that the rays are more slanting on the North Temperate Zone than on the South Temperate Zone.

Why are the rays more slanting on one zone than on the other? To find the answer, let's look at the way the earth spins.

The earth is tilted as it spins.

Let's see what is meant by "tilt." The globe in your classroom may look like this one. You can see that the North Pole and the South Pole are not right under each other.

The rod that holds the globe is tilted a little. This rod is called the axis. The classroom globe spins around its axis.

The earth, too, spins around its axis. The earth's axis is not a rod, of course. It is the center line around which the earth spins.

Sun's rays

The earth's axis is at a slant to the sunlight. The earth spins at a slant to the sunlight. The slant, or tilt, is always the same, without a wiggle or wobble. This tilt is the reason why one part of the earth has summer while another part has winter. Let's see how this happens.

More Slant, Less Heat

If you did the experiment on page 151, you found that slanting rays of sunlight give less heat than vertical rays. A place that gets slanting sunlight is usually cooler than a place that gets vertical sunlight. Slanting rays bring winter weather; vertical rays bring summer weather.

Now let's look at the earth. Let's see which parts receive the sunlight at a slant, and which parts receive it more nearly vertically.

Look at the earth in the December position. You can see that the northern part is tilted away from the sun's vertical rays.

The southern part is tilted toward the vertical rays.

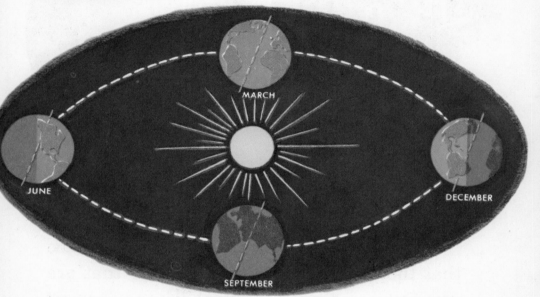

Because of this tilt, the sun's rays do not strike the two temperate zones in the same way. The tilt carries the North Temperate Zone away from the more nearly vertical rays of the sun. Here it is winter.

It carries the South Temperate Zone into the more nearly vertical rays. It is summer in the South Temperate Zone.

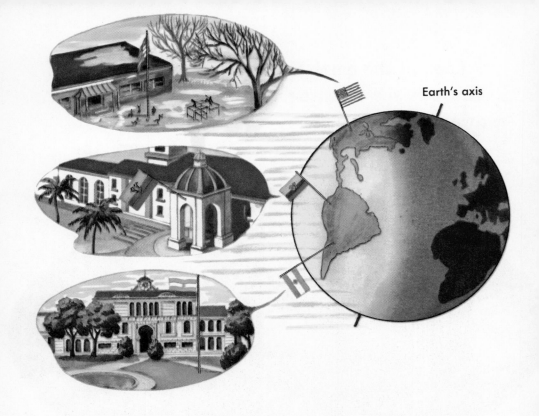

Earth's axis

Let's look at the other zones. You can see that the Torrid Zone is getting rays that are vertical or almost vertical. It is having summer weather.

The North Frigid Zone is getting no rays at all. This is the season of the long winter darkness.

The South Frigid Zone is in the sunlight. But it is a very slanting sunlight. This is the summer season in this zone, but you can see that it is a cool summer indeed.

Changing Seasons

Here is the earth in its March position. It is traveling steadily along its orbit. The slant of the axis remains the same. But as the earth moves, there is a slow change in the way it receives the rays of sunlight.

In the North Temperate Zone the sunlight strikes the earth more vertically and the winter season changes to spring.

In the South Temperate Zone the sunlight strikes the earth less vertically and the summer changes to fall.

The Torrid Zone still receives the same amount of vertical hot rays. It is still summer weather there.

The North Frigid Zone is moving into its cool summer, while the South Frigid Zone is going into its long, dark winter days.

Now look at the earth in June. How have the seasons changed?

You see that the North Frigid Zone has moved into its cool summer season.

Earth

Sun

The North Temperate Zone, too, is having summer, but the rays are more vertical and warm.

The Torrid Zone, as usual, is having the most vertical rays and the hottest weather.

The South Temperate Zone has moved into the slanting rays of winter.

The South Frigid Zone has settled down into long, dark winter.

Around and around goes the earth, spinning on its tilted axis, traveling around the sun.

The spinning carries you into sunlight and daytime, then out of the sunlight into nighttime.

The tilt of the axis brings opposite seasons to the northern and southern halves of the world. And as the earth travels around the sun it carries you into one season after another. Spinning through day and night, traveling through summer, autumn, winter, and spring, the earth goes on its never-ending journey in the sunlight.

Things to Talk About

1. Look at the picture on page 235. Find the position of the earth on the date nearest your birthday. Tell about the seasons in different parts of the world on that date.

2. Tell what things you like best about each season of the year.

3. Talk about how our seasons would be different if the earth's axis were not tilted.

4. Talk about the habits of some of the animals in your community at different seasons.

Things to Do

1. Make a model like the picture on page 235. The globes can be made of rubber balls or of clay. A knitting needle makes a good axis. Use a board for the base. Drill four slanting holes in it to support the knitting needles.

2. On a globe, take an imaginary trip from your town to each of these places: the North Pole, the South Pole, the Panama Canal, Argentina, Australia, South Africa. Through which zones do you travel? What is the season at each place?

3. Collect travel posters of foreign lands. Talk about the change of seasons in each land.

4. Make a list of the games that you play in each season of the year.

Things to Find Out

1. In your local newspaper, find out the times of sunrise and sunset. Do this every day for two weeks. Is the time of daylight becoming longer or shorter? What change in season is taking place?

2. Find out about the seasons in the North Frigid Zone and in the South Frigid Zone. Find out about the seasons in the Torrid Zone.

3. When a ship crosses the equator, there is a special ceremony for the people who are crossing for the first time. Find out about this ceremony. Perhaps you and your classmates will want to act out part of it. You will find out why you cannot act out the whole ceremony in your classroom.

4. Find out about Daylight Saving Time. Why is it used in summer and not used in winter?

WE USE POWER

Muscle Power

Long ago all the work of the world was done by human muscle. Muscles pulled the plows, hauled the water, and dragged the heavy loads.

Then people found out how to tame and train animals to work for them. Still it was slow, heavy work for muscles. People looked for other kinds of power to work for them.

Using Wind

The wind has power. Catch the wind and it will work for you. Who was it that first thought of a way to put the wind to work? No one knows. Perhaps it was a man who stood up in his little log boat and felt the wind pushing against his back. Perhaps he thought of putting up an animal skin on a stick to catch the wind.

Once, whole fleets of ships were driven by the wind. Now there are few sailing ships, and most of these are used for sport.

You can see the wind work.

EXPERIMENT

You can make a little boat yourself, and see it catch the wind. The wind can be your own breath.

First blow on the boat itself, without a sail, to see how far it goes with one long breath.

Then put up a little sail and try again. Does the boat go farther with or without the sail?

On land, too, we put the wind to work. We catch it in the blades of a windmill. The wind whirls the blades, and the blades turn a machine. The machine can be one that grinds grain, or pumps water, or generates electricity, or does some other kind of useful work.

EXPERIMENT

Make a little windmill yourself. Cut a circle out of one side of a milk carton. Then make two lines across the circle.

Cut the lines like this:

Bend them like this:

Push a sharpened toothpick through like this:

Now blow and watch the blades whirl.

How is your little windmill like a real one? How is it different?

Sometimes the wind stops blowing. Then the sailboats stop going and the windmills stop whirling. We cannot depend on wind power. Is there some other kind of power that is more sure?

Somebody, long ago, asked that question. Looking at a river flowing along, he found the answer.

Most rivers keep flowing all the time. The river water, as it moves along, has plenty of power to move things. It can carry heavy logs. It can move big boats. It can push the blades of a water wheel and make it turn. Here is an old-time water wheel. The wheel turned a machine that sawed logs.

The water wheel can turn a machine that grinds corn, or another machine that pumps water, or another that weaves cloth.

Here is a way to see water power at work turning a little wheel. Just take the little windmill you made and hold the points of the shaft lightly under a stream of water.

Now it has become a water wheel. Watch it whirl as the water hits the blades. Watch the little toothpick shaft whirl, too. If the shaft were joined to a tiny machine, it could make the machine turn, too. Then the water power would do a tiny bit of work.

EXPERIMENT

Here is a way to make your water wheel lift a little weight. Tie a small button to one end of a piece of thread. Tie the other end of the thread to the shaft of your water wheel.

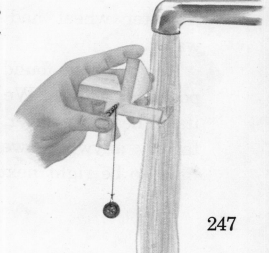

Then hold the wheel in a stream of water. The blades turn, the shaft turns, and the thread winds up and lifts the weight.

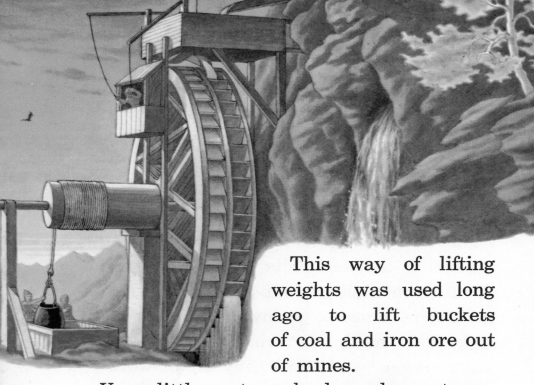

This way of lifting weights was used long ago to lift buckets of coal and iron ore out of mines.

Your little water wheel needs a stream of water to turn it, of course. A big water wheel needs a large stream of water. That is why mills had to be built near a river. Any factory whose machines were turned by a water wheel had to be near plenty of water.

Now we have found a better way to use the power of water. We build the water wheel itself near the river, but we can build the factory anywhere we want to. It does not have to be right next to the water wheel.

We Use Electric Power

This is how the moving water can turn the machines in a factory, even if the factory is far from the water.

The water turns a huge water wheel called a turbine. The shaft of the turbine also turns, just as your little toothpick shaft turned. The turbine shaft turns a big machine called an electric generator.

Electric generator

Water

Turbine

When the electric generator is turned, electricity flows out of it. The electricity goes through wires that go to the faraway factories. In the factories the electricity turns electric motors that drive many kinds of machines. There are machines that weave cloth, machines that make furniture, machines that mix dough — many kinds of useful machines.

This is a much better way of using water power. We do not have to build the mills or factories right next to a river. We can build them in any place that suits us. We can string wires from the electric generator to any place, near or far.

The electricity runs our vacuum cleaners, electric refrigerators, and many other machines. It gives light in electric lamps and heat in electric toasters and irons. In hundreds of different ways, we use the electricity made by faraway water power.

It is easy to see how a turning water wheel can turn a machine and make it work for us. But how can electricity make something turn?

You can find out by building a little electric motor. You can build it in a few minutes.

An Electric Motor

EXPERIMENT

You can build an electric motor yourself. You will need

an oatmeal box top

a pencil with an eraser tip

a spool, a small sewing needle, a snap fastener

4 paper clips

1 large nail or screw

1 dry cell

about three feet of bell wire.

Bell wire is thin copper wire covered with cotton, rubber, or plastic.

First, put the needle, pencil, and spool together like this.

Make a tiny hole in the middle of the box top. Put the tiny head of one part of the snap fastener into this hole, from underneath. Then snap the other part over the tiny head, as shown in the picture.

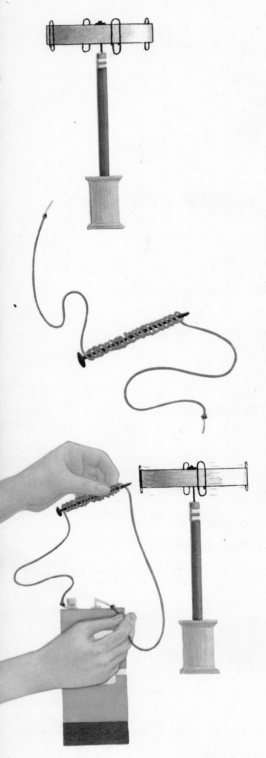

Put the four paper clips on the rim of the box top. Then place the box top with the snap fastener on the needle. Now it looks like this.

Scrape off an inch of the covering from each end of the wire. Then wrap the wire around the large nail or screw, leaving about six inches free at each end.

Bend one end of the wire around one screw of the dry cell, and fasten it. Hold the nail near one of the paper clips. Now touch the second end of the wire to the other screw of the cell. Be sure you use a dry cell and not regular house current for your motor.

Watch the box top begin to turn! Electric power is making it turn!

Before you make it spin faster, let's stop and think about what happened.

When you touched the second end of the wire to the other screw of the dry cell, electricity began to flow. It flowed out of one part of the dry cell, through the wire and back into another part of the dry cell.

When electricity flows through a wire, the wire becomes a sort of magnet! And when electricity flows through a wire around a nail it makes the nail become a magnet, too. The wire and nail together are called an electromagnet.

The electromagnet pulls the paper clip. This pull makes the box top turn.

Electromagnet

253

Now let's see how we can make the box top keep turning. To do this you have to touch the second wire to the other screw of the dry cell and then take it away. Touch and take away, touch and take away. Each touch makes the electromagnet pull one of the paper clips. Each take-away makes the electromagnet stop pulling.

You will have to practice the touch and take away until you get it just right. Then your little electric motor will keep on turning, around and around.

You can make your motor do a little work for you. Cut little paper animals and fasten them to the box top, as in the picture. Now you have a tiny electric merry-go-round!

How simple your electric motor is! Yet a real electric motor works in the same way. Even the huge, powerful motors that run the speedy elevators in tall office buildings work in the same way.

In every electric motor, big or little, there is an electromagnet, like your nail and coil of wire. There is a part that is pulled and turned by the electromagnet, like the paper clips and the box top. And, of course, there is electricity to make it go.

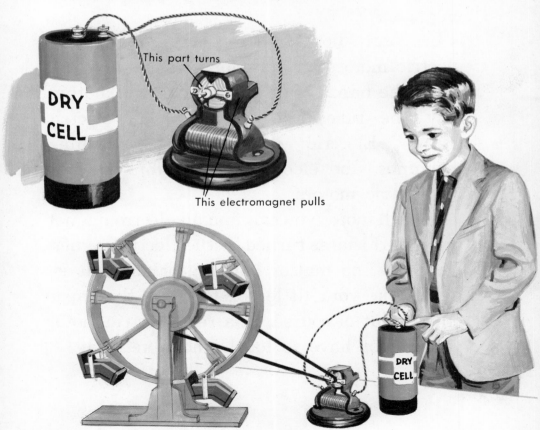

This part turns

This electromagnet pulls

Most of the electric motors you use do not use electricity from a dry cell. They use electricity from a generator. In most of our homes the electric current is a kind called A.C., which stands for alternating current. In some homes, apartments, offices, and factories the current is D.C., which stands for direct current. Some motors and other electrical appliances work with either kind of current, but others will work with only one kind. An electric clock motor runs only on A.C.

In your home there may be several electric motors at work for you. A tiny one turns the hands of an electric clock. Another tiny one turns the wheels of an electric train. Electric mixers, fans, washing machines, and electric refrigerators are run by electric motors.

In each motor you can find an electromagnet and a part that is turned by the electromagnet. Each one, no matter how big or small it is, works like your little box top with the paper clips! But of course, in a real electric motor you do not have to touch and take away!

Each one uses the power of electricity to work for you, doing jobs that would be hard and tiresome if you had to do them by muscle power.

We Use Steam Power

Another very useful kind of power is steam power. Hot steam can push with great force. It can turn a steam engine, and the steam engine can run many kinds of machines.

Perhaps you have seen steam move the lid of a teakettle.

Put a potato on the spout of a teakettle so that all the steam pushes against the lid. Watch the lid jump up and down.

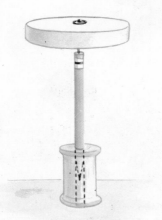

EXPERIMENT

You can build a little engine that will work by steam power. It is called a steam turbine.

First build the part that looks like this.

It is like a part of the electric motor shown on page 252.

Now cut eight strips of metal foil. Each strip is two inches long and a half inch wide. Metal foil is often used for wrapping foods; you may find some in the kitchen.

Fasten the strips of metal foil to the box top, using paper clips or staples.

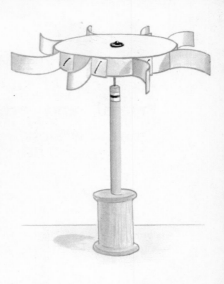

Now your steam turbine is ready to work. All you need is some steam to push against the metal foil blades of the turbine. You can get the steam by boiling some water in a teakettle. Steam will come out of the spout. Hold the turbine so that the steam pushes against the blades. Watch the turbine spin.

Real steam turbines are not built out of box tops, of course. They are made of strong metal and are much bigger. There are many wheels. But they work in the same way as your little steam turbine.

Steam from boiling water flows against the blades of the turbine and makes it spin rapidly.

A steam turbine

Steam pushes against blades.

The spinning turbine is joined to another machine that can do useful work for us.

For instance, if it is joined to an electric generator, it causes the generator to spin, and electricity is made. Then the electricity can go through wires to places where it is needed. This is the most common way of getting electricity, and it is used in the many places where there is not enough water power to spin the big generators.

The steam turbine can be joined to a ship's propeller. It causes the propeller to spin. The spinning propeller pushes the ship forward through the water.

No matter what sort of work a steam turbine does, or how big it is, you will always find the same main parts. There is a fire to heat water and make it boil into steam. Usually there are wheels with blades against which the steam pushes.

Gasoline Engines

Steam turbines are not used for driving a car or airplane. They are too heavy, and they take too long to "get up steam" and get ready to go. But there is another kind of engine that does not weigh so much, and that starts quickly. For cars and planes, a gasoline engine works well.

The power of a gasoline engine comes from the burning of gasoline. When gasoline or any other fuel burns it gives off gases and it heats up the air near it. If the fuel burns in some kind of container, the heated-up air and the new gases made from the fuel press on the sides of the container. Even the fire of a little match can make a powerful pressure. You can see this for yourself, with a few simple materials and some patience.

EXPERIMENT

You will need a magnifying glass, two small matches, and a small medicine bottle with a plain stopper. Remember, it must have a plain stopper and not a screw top.

Put the matches in the bottle, with their tips together. Wet the stopper and put it in the neck of the bottle. Put it in loosely; don't jam it in. Put it in the sunlight, with the stopper facing away from you.

Hold the magnifying glass so that the sunlight comes to a point on one of the match tips. In about a minute or so the matches catch fire. As they burn, they give off hot gases under pressure. Watch the stopper fly off with a pop!

Now let's see how the power of fire can run an engine. It's too hard to set up a real experiment; so let's do an imaginary experiment with the medicine bottle. Let's imagine that we use a stopper that can slide inside the bottle. We attach one end of a rod to the stopper. The other end is attached to a bent piece called a crank, with a wheel.

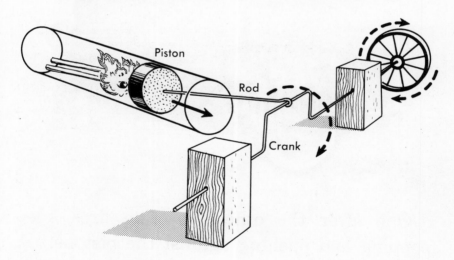

Now, if we set fire to the matches, the hot gases will push out the stopper. The stopper pushes the rod, and the rod turns the crank and the wheel. We have used the power of fire to run an engine.

The gasoline engine in a car, bus, or plane works in the same way. Instead of burning matches, it burns gasoline. The "medicine bottle" is much larger and is made of strong metal. Usually there are several of them in an engine. The "stopper" is a round metal part called a piston. Each piston has a rod that is joined to a crank. Each piston is pushed by the pressure of hot gases from a gasoline fire.

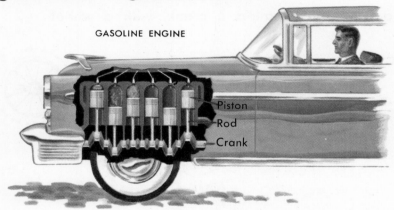

GASOLINE ENGINE

Piston
Rod
Crank

One after the other, gasoline fires keep popping and pushing against the pistons. A special part keeps sending in more gasoline to burn. The pressure of the hot gases gives the power to turn the wheels of a car or the propeller of an airplane.

Diesel Engines

Some trucks, trains, and boats are run by diesel engines. A diesel engine is like a gasoline engine in most ways. Its power comes from puffs of fire, but it burns oil instead of gasoline. Diesel engines are very good for pulling big, heavy loads.

In diesel engines and gasoline engines, fire works for us, quickly and easily. The power of fire has been used by people to do jobs that would be slow and hard for muscles to do.

We use power machines in many ways, yet we hardly ever think about it. Let's think about it for a minute. Think about this Indian boy, who lived long ago when there were no power machines.

His clothing was of buffalo skin. His food was buffalo meat and corn, and very little else. If the hunters found no buffaloes, if the rains did not come to water the corn, the winter would be a time of hunger.

Getting food, building homes, making clothes, and keeping warm was long, hard work for everyone, because everything had to be done with muscles.

Life is very different for this boy. Plenty
of food grows on his father's farm, with
enough left over for people in faraway cities.
He wears better clothes and lives in a more
comfortable home. The work is easier, with
more time to play, to study, and to rest.

What made all the difference? Many
things, but most of all, power machines.
Power machines now do most of the heavy
work that muscles used to do. Power on the
farm and in the city, in factories, and in
homes, has helped to make life more
pleasant and comfortable for us all.

267

Things to Talk About

1. Talk about the kind of power that was used in building each of these two houses. Talk about the kind of power that is used by the people living in each house for cooking, cleaning, heating, lighting, and other things.

2. Talk about how power has changed travel.

3. Talk about how your life would be changed if electric power were cut off for a few days.

Things to Do

1. Make a picture chart of animals that carry burdens for people. Try to show some animals used in faraway lands.

2. Collect pictures of waterfalls. Tell which ones you think would be good for power.

3. Make steam ring a bell. Tape a light stick to the knob on the cover of a teakettle. Tie a little bell to the other end of the stick. Put a potato over the spout of the kettle and heat water in the kettle. When the water boils, the steam will push the cover up and down. This will ring the bell.

4. On an outline map of the United States put in important railroad routes, big waterways, and main airline routes. Use different-colored crayons for each way of travel.

Things to Find Out

1. Find out whether it is cheaper to make electricity by falling water or by steam. Give some reasons.

2. Find out about the difference in cost of shipping a large crate by boat, by train, and by airplane. Give some reasons.

3. Find out about some cargo that is usually shipped by water.

4. Find out the source of electricity in your community.

5. Find out where gasoline comes from.

6. Find out the difference between regular gasoline and ethyl gasoline.

TRAVELERS AROUND THE SUN

You Are a Traveler

Do you know that you are a great traveler? From yesterday until today you traveled almost two million miles! Without getting into a car, or boat, or plane, you travel millions of miles every day.

You ride on the earth as it circles around the sun. Steadily and evenly, without a bump or shake, never stopping for a traffic light, your earth has carried you many millions of miles since you were born.

Perhaps you have wondered why you cannot feel the swift movement of the earth. You can feel the movement of a car or boat, yet they go much more slowly.

Cars and boats do not ride smoothly. You can feel them bump and shake. You can hear the sound of wheels and engines. You can see things whizzing by.

You know you are moving because you see, hear, or feel motion.

The earth's movement is silent and steady and smooth. You cannot feel yourself moving. You cannot see or hear the moving.

No wonder people used to think that the earth stands still! They could not feel or hear any motion.

When they looked at the sky they could see motion, but it seemed to be the motion of other things and not the earth.

They could see the sun, and it seemed to move from east to west every day.

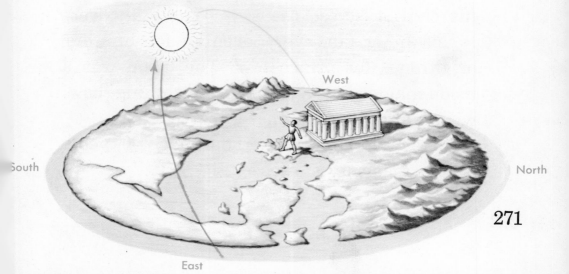

West

South

North

East

They could see the moon seem to travel across the sky. The stars, too, seemed to move. All this movement was really the turning of the earth, but people of long ago had no way of knowing this.

Because the people could not tell what was really happening, they made up all kinds of stories to explain what they saw.

They said the sun was a fire-god rolling in his chariot across the sky. The stars were lamps hung out every evening for hunters, or thrones for princesses. The moon was a moon-maiden, or a man, or a shining bowl with water to pour on the earth.

In every land, for thousands of years people made up stories of the sky.

Stories, however, are not enough. They may be wonderful to listen to and think about, but they are stories. Some people wanted to know more, and, bit by bit, they found out.

With telescopes and with other instruments, scientists found out that the sun is a huge, fiery ball, much larger than the earth.

They saw the rocky plains and mountains of the moon.

They found that the stars are glowing globes like our sun, and that most of the stars are bigger than our sun.

They found out, too, that the sun does not travel around the earth. It is the earth that travels around the sun.

How strange and frightening these discoveries must have seemed at first!

Strangest and most frightening of all was the idea that the earth was whirling and spinning swiftly around the sun. The scientists had found that this was true, but many people refused to believe it.

However, the scientists continued to explore the skies. They built larger telescopes. They invented other instruments for studying the sky. And the more they watched and studied, the more certain they became that the earth is not the center of all the heavenly bodies. They felt sure that the earth spins steadily on its axis as it travels around the sun.

The earth is important to us because we live on it. It does not have to be the center of everything to be important.

We are safe on the earth. Even though the earth moves swiftly through space, we cannot fall off.

Gravity

"Hold tight, we're going around a curve!"
You have to hold tight to stay on a
merry-go-round. But you do not have to hold
tight to stay on the bigger merry-go-round,
the earth.

The earth holds you tight. When you try
to jump away, the earth pulls you right back.
The earth never stops pulling. It pulls all
the time, everywhere, on every single thing.

The pull of the earth is called gravity.

Look at a rubber ball lying on the floor. It has a round shape, and it is made of a certain amount of rubber. Now pick up the ball and hold it in your hand. Is the ball any different?

The shape of the ball is the same; the amount of material is the same. But in a way that you cannot see, the ball is different. It can do something that it couldn't do when it lay on the floor. It can fall.

Perhaps this sounds like a joke and not a very good one. But it is a serious problem of science. It is one that has puzzled scientists for thousands of years.

And there is as yet no sure answer to the simple question, "What makes the ball fall when you let it go?"

Oh, yes, we say the earth's gravity pulls it. But just what does that mean? With what kind of invisible thread does the earth pull the ball?

There is no thread, there is no anything, but in some way or other the earth pulls. And nobody is sure exactly how it happens.

Even though we don't know how gravity works, we use it all the time.

When you pull a sled to the top of a hill, you do so because you are counting on gravity to do its part, to pull you down the hill.

When you throw a ball up into the air, you are not afraid that the ball will sail off into space. You know that gravity will bring the ball down to your waiting hands.

In hundreds of different ways, you use gravity all the time, and it never fails you.

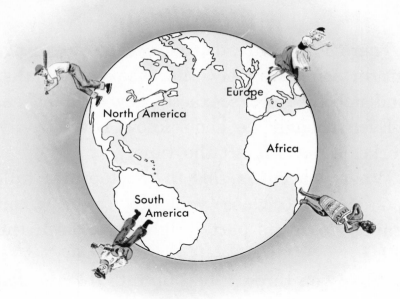

Who's Upside Down?

Everybody in place! Gravity is holding everybody in place on the earth. But some of the people seem to be standing in the wrong way. Some people seem to be standing sideways. Others seem upside down. Doesn't everything look queer to them?

Not at all. Each one sees the sky above his head and the ground under his feet.

So everything looks right to everybody.

Everything feels right, too. You can feel that you are standing the right way, even with your eyes shut. That is because you feel gravity pulling you toward the ground.

Everybody else feels right side up, too. Everybody else feels pulled toward the ground. Everywhere the pull of gravity is toward the earth.

No matter where you go, "down" is toward the earth and "up" is away from the earth.

Is this boy upside down or right side up? Tell why.

What does the boy see that tells him he is upside down?

What does he feel that tells him he is upside down?

The Moon

The earth's gravity pulls everything, all the time. It pulls tiny grains of sand; it pulls you; it pulls huge, heavy buildings. And it pulls something much bigger and heavier, the moon.

The moon is a huge, heavy ball of rock. On the moon there are mountains and valleys and wide, rocky deserts.

There is no water or air on the moon and there are no living things. Silent and alone, without the sound of life, without wind or wave to change it, the moon circles endlessly around the earth.

The earth's gravity pulls the heavy moon. It helps to keep the moon circling around the earth. The moon takes about four weeks to travel all the way around the earth.

As the moon travels, sunlight shines upon it. That is why we can see the moon.

Sunlight on the earth makes daylight. Sunlight on the moon makes moonlight.

The Moon and Tides

The earth's gravity pulls the moon. The moon has gravity, too, and it pulls the earth. But the moon is much smaller and lighter than the earth, so its gravity is much weaker.

Even so, the pull of the moon's gravity does something to the earth. It makes tides.

If you have been to the seashore, you know that the level of the water changes from time to time. Sometimes the ocean is high, so that it flows in and covers a good part of the beach. This is the time of high tide.

At other times the ocean is low. At low tide, much of the beach is left uncovered. You see clams, mussels, and other water animals left sticking out.

The ocean heaps up into high tide and then it sinks into low tide. This heaping up and sinking is caused by the moon's gravity.

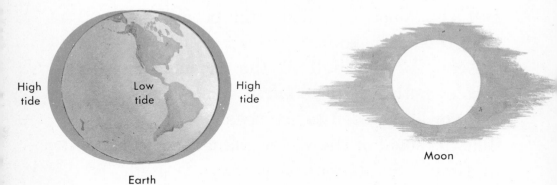

High tide   Low tide   High tide

Earth   Moon

The moon's gravity pulls the nearest water a little away from the earth. This causes a high tide on the side of the earth facing the moon. The water on the opposite side is farthest from the moon. This water gets the weakest pull of the moon's gravity, so it is left heaped up in a bulge. This bulge is the other high tide on the earth. Between the two bulges are the two low tides.

Because the earth keeps turning, the high tides keep traveling around the earth. The high tides come about every twelve and a half hours in the oceans all over the earth, with low tides between.

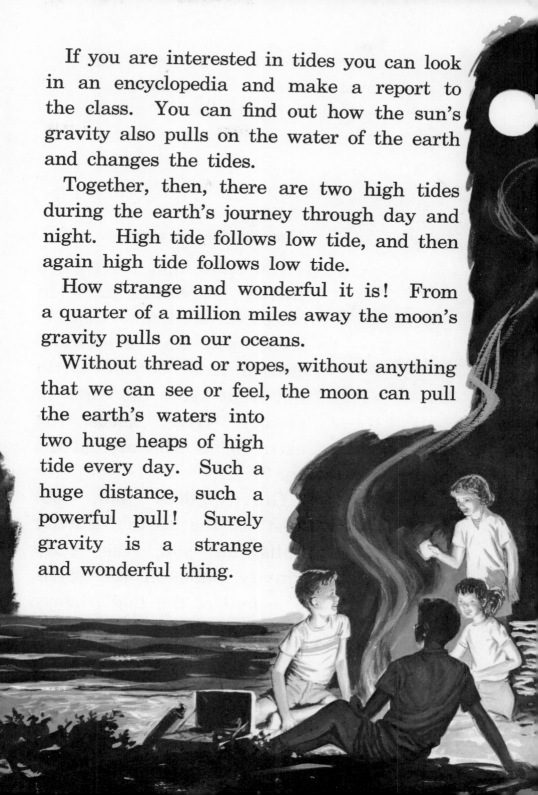

If you are interested in tides you can look in an encyclopedia and make a report to the class. You can find out how the sun's gravity also pulls on the water of the earth and changes the tides.

Together, then, there are two high tides during the earth's journey through day and night. High tide follows low tide, and then again high tide follows low tide.

How strange and wonderful it is! From a quarter of a million miles away the moon's gravity pulls on our oceans.

Without thread or ropes, without anything that we can see or feel, the moon can pull the earth's waters into two huge heaps of high tide every day. Such a huge distance, such a powerful pull! Surely gravity is a strange and wonderful thing.

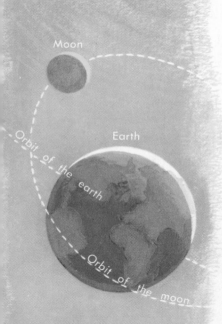

Moon

Earth

Orbit of the earth

Orbit of the moon

The Sun's Gravity

You know that the earth's gravity keeps the moon in place. You know that it keeps you and everything else in place on the earth. But what keeps the earth in place? What keeps the earth in its orbit around the sun?

Gravity does that, too! Just as the earth's gravity pulls on you, the sun's gravity pulls on the earth. The pull of the huge, heavy sun keeps the earth in its orbit.

Things to Talk About

1. Talk about how gravity works for you. For example, you might talk about "Gravity in a Baseball Game" or "Gravity at an Amusement Park."

2. Take a little doll for a walk around a globe. Walk it from the North Pole to the South Pole and back again. Talk about up and down at different places on the trip.

3. When you ride in a car, you have several ways of knowing that you are in motion. Talk about these ways. How do you know in a train? In an elevator? In an airplane? On an escalator? How is the earth's motion different from the motion of any of these?

4. Imagine that you are in a space ship far out in space with no gravity pulling you. Talk about some of the things you could not do. For example, you could not pour water from a pitcher into a cup. Why not?

Things to Do

1. Look at the moon through field glasses or a telescope. You can see mountains and craters even with low-powered glasses.

2. With two of your classmates act out the motions of the earth and moon around the sun.

3. Make a picture chart called "Gravity at Work." The pictures on page 277 will give you some ideas to start with.

Things to Find Out

1. Find out some of the stories that people have made up about the stars. For example, how did the Great Bear get its name?

2. Two men who are famous for their discoveries about gravity are Galileo and Isaac Newton. Find out about the work of these men.

3. If you live near the sea or the Great Lakes, find out the times of high tide and low tide each day for a week. You can usually find this information in a newspaper. How do the times change from day to day?

4. Find out why ship captains are interested in tides.

5. Find out about the two kinds of telescopes called reflectors and refractors.

6. An airplane pilot sometimes wears a suit called an Anti-G Suit to keep him from blacking out in a sudden turn or a fast dive. Find out why the suit is called an Anti-G Suit.

NEIGHBORS IN SPACE

URANUS · JUPITER · MARS MERCURY · VENUS EARTH SATURN NEPTUNE PLUTO

The earth has company in its travels. Other globes like the earth also circle around the sun. These globes and the earth are called planets.

Each planet travels in its own path, called its orbit, held in place by the sun's gravity.

Some of the planets travel closer to the sun than we do. Others are farther away. Some are smaller than the earth, while others are much larger.

Some have one or more moons traveling around them. Others have none. All together the planets, moons, and sun make up a family called the solar system.

287

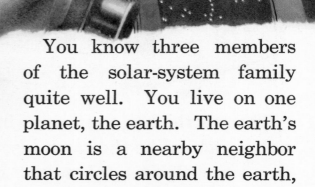

You know three members of the solar-system family quite well. You live on one planet, the earth. The earth's moon is a nearby neighbor that circles around the earth, much as the earth circles around the sun.

You also know the sun itself, and you know that the heat and light of the earth come from the sun.

Other members of the solar system are less known to you, because they appear too small or are too far away.

Someone may have pointed out the nearer planets to you, such as Mercury, Venus, Mars, Jupiter, and Saturn. These look like stars. You would need a telescope to see the farther planets, Uranus, Neptune, and Pluto.

All Aboard the Space Ship!

Have you ever wondered what it would be like to live on another planet? Have you wondered whether you would find other living things there?

Nowadays, with huge telescopes and other instruments, we are finding out things about our neighbor planets. Someday, perhaps, we shall learn still more about these planets. We may even have rocket ships that will streak through empty space at terrific speeds, carrying explorers from the earth. What would such a voyage be like? What would explorers find?

Space

The trip in a rocket ship would surely be a strange experience.

All your life you have lived with the earth's gravity at work on you, pulling you toward the ground. Out in space you would have a hard time getting used to living without the earth's gravity.

Without gravity, you would have to move carefully in the space ship. The least little jump would send you sailing off the floor on  your way toward a bump against the ceiling. Sitting or lying down would be a problem, without gravity to keep you on your chair or bed. How would you take a drink of water without gravity to make the water flow into your mouth? If you let go of the glass, it would not fall; it would just stay there in space! You would also have to remember to put your arms down. Without gravity to pull them down, your arms would stay in whatever position you happened to leave them. Life in a space ship would certainly be queer for you.

Visit to Mercury

Life on another planet would be even more queer than life in the space ship. Let's pretend that we have landed on Mercury.

Mercury is the planet that is nearest to the sun. It is much closer to the sun than the earth is. Mercury is not even half so far from the hot sun as we are. Being as close to the sun as that, Mercury is very hot on its daytime side. We believe this side to be so hot that it can melt lead. Better put on your heatproof suit!

You will need your oxygen helmet and tank as well, for there is no air on Mercury. The suit, helmet, and tank were very heavy when you tried them on back on Earth. Here they feel much lighter. Here on Mercury, the gravity is much weaker. You hardly know that you have the thick suit on as you go leaping about in thirty-foot jumps.

Don't forget your supply of drinking water. Do you expect to find brooks and pleasant lakes on a planet whose temperature goes over 600 degrees? Six hundred degrees! Let's not stay on Mercury. Let's try another planet.

Venus

Venus is nearby, the second planet from the sun. Be prepared for surprises, because nobody has ever seen the surface of Venus.

Dense layers of clouds hide the view. These are not clouds of water droplets, but are clouds of some other materials — poisonous gases!

Venus

There is no oxygen, so be sure to have your oxygen tank and helmet in place. Here they will feel heavy, for the gravity of Venus is almost the same as it is on the earth.

The temperature, however, is probably almost the same as the earth's, so you won't have to wear your heavy, heatproof suit.

When you land on Venus, be sure to make notes and take pictures of everything you see. You will be the first person from the earth to see more of Venus than its layer of clouds, so everybody back home on the earth will be eager to learn what you find out.

Earth

We have visited the first planet, Mercury, and the second planet, Venus. Now let's think about the third planet from the sun, Earth.

Is the temperature on the earth right for living things? Is there enough oxygen for them to breathe? Is there water on the earth? Do you think there are living things on the earth?

Mars

The fourth planet, Mars, is probably the most interesting of all. There is a better chance of finding living things here than on any other planet except Earth. The temperature on Mars is almost the same as that on the earth.

There may be a little oxygen and water vapor in the air on Mars. Scientists have seen white caps on the north and south poles of Mars. After long study through powerful telescopes, they have decided that these may be snow. These white caps slowly shrink and disappear during summer on Mars. If you land on Mars in your space ship, you can tell us what the white caps are on close view. You can also find out about the green patches that sometimes change to brown. Are they plants that grow and die every season? If not, what are they? Be sure to take notes. Collect some samples if you can, and bring them back with you.

You will have a little trouble getting used to Mars' gravity. It is only about one fourth as strong as the earth's, so you can jump four times as far and high. When you have enjoyed the jumping for a while, stop and take notes of everything that you see.

Scientists think there may be plant life and perhaps even animal life on Mars. Be sure to find out and let us know.

Jupiter

When you reach the fifth planet, Jupiter, you will be satisfied just to say hello and good-by. Everything about Jupiter seems to be wrong for you. There are dense clouds, which scientists think may be composed of ammonia. Have you ever smelled kitchen ammonia? How would you like clouds of that harsh material all around you?

The gravity on Jupiter is enormous. That is because it is the largest and heaviest planet, much larger than the earth. The enormous gravity makes every part of you seem terribly heavy.

If you weigh 100 pounds on the earth, you feel almost three times as heavy on Jupiter. That is as heavy as a huge, fat man. But your muscles are no stronger; so you can barely drag yourself across the ground.

It is very, very cold, because Jupiter is very far from the sun. Your heated space suit seems to weigh a ton, and your oxygen tank and helmet weigh you down still more.

How glad you are to drag yourself back into your space ship!

You press the button to start the engine. There is a moment of fear as nothing seems to happen. Has the engine frozen in the bitter cold? Then there is a welcome roar, and with a whoosh you are off.

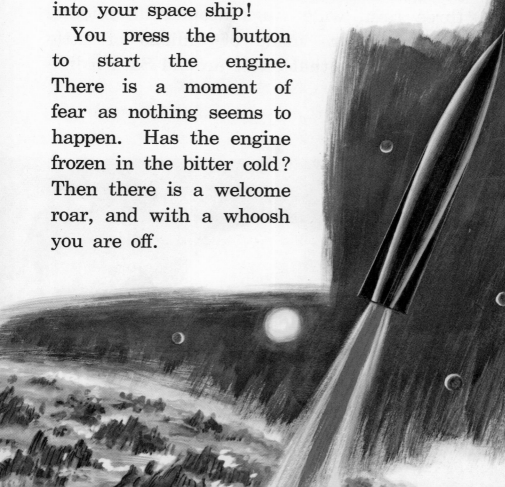

That fright you had on Jupiter was quite enough. You decide to read about the other planets before deciding where to go next. In a book about the solar system that you have with you in the space ship, you find out more facts.

Saturn

From your book you learn that the sixth planet, Saturn, is quite beautiful. It has three thin, wide rings around its middle. The rings are made of billions of little pieces of rock that circle around Saturn like little moons.

Perhaps these rings are worth visiting, you think, and then you read further. You find out that the air on Saturn has no oxygen but does have plenty of poisonous gas.

The temperature on Saturn is very, very cold, about 200 degrees below zero. This is no place for you, or any other living thing.

Uranus

The seventh planet, Uranus, is another good place to stay away from. It is even colder than Saturn, and its thick layer of clouds contains no oxygen. This thick layer cuts off most of the sunlight, so you would have to grope your way in almost complete darkness. No trip to Uranus for you!

Neptune

You would not care for Neptune, either. Neptune has no oxygen, and it is a fearfully cold, gloomy place, under its thick layer of clouds. Nothing could live here or want to live here.

Pluto

The ninth planet, Pluto, is so far away that we can barely see it with a powerful telescope. It is smaller than the earth, and is so far from the sun that it must be too cold even to think about. It is better to read about Pluto than to visit it.

Home Again

After reading about these farther planets you decide they are not for you and you head your space ship homeward. Soon you are home on Earth again! Your trip to the planets of our solar system is over. As you take off your space suit and sit down to a hot meal, you feel sure about a few things.

1. It is very, very unlikely that there is life on any other planet in our solar system, except perhaps Mars.
2. For people who live on the earth, there is no better place to live than the earth.
3. There is enough exploring left to do on the earth to keep scientists busy far, far into the future. There's room for you if you want to explore, too.

Things to Talk About

1. Make believe that the sun stopped shining. (Of course this won't really happen.) Talk about some of the changes that would take place on the earth.

2. Have you ever been to a planetarium or an observatory? Tell about your visit.

3. The gravity on Mars is about one fourth as much as the gravity on Earth. A person who weighs 100 pounds on Earth would weigh about 25 pounds on Mars. Imagine an athletic competition on Mars with contests in running, jumping, and weight-lifting. Describe some of these contests.

Things to Do

1. Is there a telescope in your community? Perhaps you can arrange to look through it.

2. Make clay ball models of the planets. Use the pictures on this page as a guide for size. Which planet is the largest? Which is the smallest? In which size place is Earth?

MERCURY

VENUS

EARTH

MARS

JUPITER

SATURN

URANUS

NEPTUNE

PLUTO

3. Turn on a bright electric light without a shade. Hold a thermometer two feet away. Keep it there for two minutes. What temperature does the thermometer show? Repeat the experiment at a distance of one foot. Then repeat it at two inches. How does this experiment help to explain the temperatures of Pluto, Earth, and Mercury?

4. Darken the room. Hold a sheet of white paper close to a lighted bulb or flashlight. Move the paper farther and farther away from the light. How does the brightness of the paper change? How does this explain the fact that Mercury appears much brighter than Saturn?

Things to Find Out

1. Find out which planets can be seen at this time of the year in your community.

2. Find out about meteors and meteorites. These are also called shooting stars and fireballs.

3. Find out what a comet is. How is it like a planet? How is it different?

Science Words

This part of the book will help you to pronounce and to understand the meanings of important science words used in the book.

The words are divided into syllables and a mark ′ is placed after the syllable which is said with the most force. The meaning fits the way the word is used on the page given in parentheses.

A. C. An abbreviation for alternating current. An electric current that flows first in one direction and then in the other, rapidly back and forth. Most electric current for houses and factories is alternating current. (p. 256)

air. A mixture of gases which surrounds the earth. Air contains oxygen, which all living things need. (p. 2)

air′plane. A flying machine with wings and a motor. (p. 25)

ant′eat er. A four-footed mammal that eats ants. It has a long, sticky tongue that reaches into anthills. (p. 161)

a quar′i um. A place where water plants and animals are kept. It may be a bowl, tank, or building. (p. 197)

ax′is. The earth's axis is an imaginary line through the earth, from the North Pole to the South Pole, around which the earth turns or rotates. (p. 232)

ax′le. A rod or shaft on which a wheel turns. (p. 45)

ball bear′ing. A ring of balls placed between an axle and the wheel that turns around it. The balls allow the wheel to turn more easily, with less friction. (p. 51)

brake. A part of a machine that is used for slowing or stopping the machine. (p. 55)

bulb. A round, fleshy, underground part of a plant. Onions, tulips, and lilies grow bulbs. New plants can grow from bulbs. (p. 112)

cell. A small, boxlike bit of material. All living things are made of cells. (p. 186)

chlo′rine. A greenish-yellow gas with a harsh, strong smell. It is used for making water safe to drink. (p. 225)

cli'mate. The kind of weather a place usually has. Heat and cold, wetness and dryness, windiness and calm are all part of climate. (p. 143)

com pressed' air. Air that has been squeezed into a smaller space. (p. 98)

crank. A handle used to turn part of a machine. (p. 263)

D. C. An abbreviation for direct current. An electric current that flows steadily in one direction. Batteries give direct current. (p. 256)

des'ert. A place which does not have enough rainfall for farming. (p. 173)

die'sel en'gine. An engine that works like an automobile engine, except that it burns oil instead of gasoline. (p. 265)

dike. An earth dam or bank to keep back water. (p. 214)

dis solve'. To become part of a liquid. Salt and sugar dissolve in water. (p. 193)

drone. A male bee. (p. 137)

dry cell. A sealed can with chemicals that can produce an electric current. (p. 251)

e las'tic. Able to spring back to its own shape and size after being stretched or squeezed. A rubber ball is elastic. (p. 93)

e lec'tric gen'er a tor. A machine for producing electricity. (p. 249)

e lec tro mag'net. A piece of iron with a coil of insulated wire around it. When an electric current is passed through the coil, the electromagnet can attract iron or steel. (p. 253)

e vap'o rate. To change into a vapor or gas. (p. 22)

ex pand'. To spread out or become larger. (p. 14)

ex per'i ment. A way of finding out by trying or testing. (p. 5)

fil'ter. To pass through a material which strains out impurities. (p. 221)

fish. An animal that lives in water, breathes through gills, has fins, and is covered with scales. (p. 61)

fog. A thick mist made of tiny drops of water. (p. 21)

fric'tion. The rubbing and dragging between two surfaces. (p. 39)

frost. Frozen dew or water vapor. (p. 21)

fu'el. Anything that can be used for burning. Coal, oil, and wood are fuels. (p. 145)

germs. Very tiny plants or animals that can cause disease. (p. 221)

glid′er. A flying machine with wings but no motor. (p. 76)

grav′i ty. The earth's gravity is the force that pulls all things to the earth. All heavenly bodies (sun, moon, planets, and stars) also have gravity. (p. 275)

hel′i cop ter. A flying machine with a motor but no wings. It is kept up by large propellers on top. (p. 83)

in′sect. A small animal with three body parts and six legs. (p. 120)

jet plane. An airplane with a special kind of engine called a jet engine. (p. 85)

Ju′pi ter. The fifth planet from the sun. It is the largest planet. (p. 287)

lu′bri cate. To make something smooth and slippery by putting on grease or oil. (p. 50)

mag′ni fy ing glass. A piece of curved glass that makes a thing look larger than it is. (p. 187)

Mars. The fourth planet from the sun. Scientists think there may be plant life and perhaps even animal life on Mars. (p. 287)

Mer′cu ry. The planet that is nearest to the sun. It is the smallest planet. (p. 287)

mi′cro scope. An instrument that makes a small thing look larger. (p. 186)

mol′e cule. The smallest particle of a substance. For example, the smallest particles of water are water molecules. (p. 23)

nec′tar. A sweet liquid found in flowers. (p. 120)

Nep′tune. The eighth planet from the sun. (p. 287)

North Frig′id Zone. The part of the earth's surface which is near the North Pole. (p. 163)

North Tem′per ate Zone. The part of the earth's surface between the North Frigid Zone and the Torrid Zone. (p. 163)

or′bit. The orbit of the earth or any other planet is its path around the sun. (p. 231)

o′vule. The part of a plant that develops into a seed. (p. 119)

ox′y gen. A gas without color or odor. It makes up part of the air. It is needed by all living things. (p. 226)

pis'til. The part of a flower that holds the seed. (p. 119)

pis'ton. A metal piece, usually shaped like a can, that slides back and forth in a machine. Steam engines and automobile engines have pistons. (p. 100)

plan'et. One of the nine large bodies that move around the sun. The earth is a planet. (p. 287)

Plu'to. The planet that is farthest from the sun. (p. 287)

pol'len. A fine powder, usually yellowish in color, found in flowers. Pollen causes ovules to develop into seeds. (p. 120)

pol lute'. To make dirty. Polluted water is not fit to drink. (p. 222)

po'rous. Having little holes through which liquids can go. (p. 199)

pro pel'ler. The part of an airplane or boat that pushes it through the air or water. Propellers have several blades around a hub. They are whirled by a motor. (p. 59)

queen bee. A female, or mother, bee. (p. 138)

res'er voir. A place where water is collected and stored for use. (p. 227)

roll'er. A part shaped like a candle or a smooth log. (p. 43)

root. The part of a plant that grows down into the soil. It holds the plant in place. It takes in water and minerals from the soil. (p. 105)

Sat'urn. The sixth planet from the sun. (p. 287)

sew'age. Waste matter from sinks and toilets, which flows into sewers. (p. 222)

soil. A mixture of crumbled rock and rotted plant material. Most of the land part of the earth is covered with soil. (p. 10)

so'lar sys'tem. The sun with the planets and their moons which travel around it. (p. 287)

South Frig'id Zone. The part of the earth's surface which is near the South Pole. (p. 163)

South Tem'per ate Zone. The part of the earth's surface between the South Frigid Zone and the Torrid Zone. (p. 163)

squid. A sea animal with ten arms and a long body. (p. 61)

stag'nant. Not moving or flowing. The water in a stagnant pool is usually not fit to drink. (p. 225)

stem. The part of a plant aboveground which supports the other parts. A tree trunk and a cornstalk are stems. (p. 105)

swamp. Wet, soft land. (p. 205)

tel'e scope. An instrument that makes faraway things seem nearer and larger. (p. 273)

tem'per a ture. The degree of heat or cold. (p. 11)

ther mom'e ter. An instrument for measuring temperature. (p. 5)

tide. The regular rise and fall of the ocean about every 12½ hours, caused by the attraction of the moon and sun. (p. 281)

Tor'rid Zone. A belt of land and sea about three thousand miles wide extending around the earth halfway between the North and South Poles. (p. 159)

trans par'ent. Easy to see through. (p. 169)

tur'bine. An engine with blades like a pinwheel. The blades are spun by the force of steam, water, air, or burning gases. A windmill and a water wheel are turbines. (p. 249)

ty'phoid fe'ver. A dangerous disease caused by germs that are sometimes found in unclean food or water. (p. 221)

U'ra nus. The seventh planet from the sun. (p. 287)

u'rine. A liquid that contains waste material from the body. Urine is collected by the kidneys and is then stored in the bladder until it is passed out of the body. (p. 183)

Ve'nus. The second planet from the sun. (p. 287)

ver'ti cal. Straight up and down, not slanting. The walls of a building are vertical. (p. 151)

wa'ter ta'ble. The top of the underground water. (p. 201)

wa'ter wheel. A wheel with blades fastened to it. The wheel is turned by flowing water. The turning of the wheel causes a machine to do work. (p. 246)

wind'mill. A machine with blades that are turned by the wind. The turning of the blades causes a pump or other machine to do work. (p. 244)

work'er bee. One of the bees that do the work in a hive. (p. 137)

Index

Seeds, 105, 115, 118–131
contain baby plants, 124–128
how they are made, 118–122
how they travel, 129–131
Sleet, how it is formed, 28
Snow
how it is formed, 30–31
on Mars, 295
traveling on it, 36–37, 40–41
why it warms more slowly than land, 154
Soda straw, how it works, 97–98
Solar system, 287–288
South Frigid Zone, 236, 238
South Pole, 233
South Temperate Zone, 233, 235, 237, 238
Space ship, an imaginary journey, 289–300
Squids, 61–62
Stars, 272, 273
Steam power, 258–261
Summer
in the far north, 143, 144, 147, 149–153, 155
what causes the heat, 5–7
See also Seasons
Sun, 288
at the North Pole, 144
the cause of winds, 13–21
early stories about it, 272
effect on climate, 147, 148–153, 159, 162–164
effect on seasons, 234–239
effect on temperature, 3–7

how the planets travel around it, 287
how we travel around it, 270–274
in summer and in winter, 5–7
its gravity, 284, 287
its size, 273
the source of heat, 2–4
why the slant of its rays varies, 232–239
Swamps, 205–208, 217
Swimming, 60–61

Telescope, 273, 288
Temperate Zones, 162, 233, 235, 237, 238
Temperature
on Earth, 294
on Jupiter, 297
on Mars, 294
on Mercury, 291, 292
on Neptune, 299
on Pluto, 300
on Saturn, 299
on Uranus, 299
on Venus, 293
Tides, 281–283
Tilt of the earth, 233–239
Tires, 93, 99
Torrid Zone, 157–159, 160–161, 236, 237, 238
Traveling
in the air, 71–89
in space, 270–274, 289–300
in water, 59–68
See also Boats
on land, see Moving things
Turbines, 249, 258–261

313